the
divorce workbook
for teens

activities to help
you **move beyond**
the **breakup**

LISA M. SCHAB, LCSW

Instant Help Books
A Division of New Harbinger Publications, Inc.

Distributed in Canada by Raincoast Books

Copyright © 2008 by Lisa M. Schab
              Instant Help Books
              A Division of New Harbinger Publications, Inc.
              5674 Shattuck Avenue
              Oakland, CA 94609
              www.newharbinger.com

Cover design by Amy Shoup
Text design by David Eustace
Illustrated by Julie Olson

ISBN 978-1-931704-27-4

Library of Congress Cataloging in Publication Data on file

Printed in the United States of America

10   09   08

10   9   8   7   6   5   4   3   2   1

First Printing

table of contents

Introduction   v

Activity 1:   Your Thoughts and Feelings   1

Activity 2:   Surviving Your Parents' Divorce   5

Activity 3:   Acting Out   10

Activity 4:   Guilt   14

Activity 5:   Fear   18

Activity 6:   Sadness and Depression   23

Activity 7:   Anger   28

Activity 8:   Grief and Loss   32

Activity 9:   Abandonment   37

Activity 10:   Neglect   43

Activity 11:   Happiness   48

Activity 12:   Confusion   52

Activity 13:   Other Feelings   57

Activity 14:   Wishing for Reconciliation   62

Activity 15:   Blaming One Parent   65

Activity 16:   Blaming the Divorce   70

Activity 17:   Your Feelings about Marriage   74

Activity 18:   Your Sexuality   78

Activity 19:   Moving   84

Activity 20:   Living in Two Homes   90

Activity 21:   Visitation   95

Activity 22:   Finances   101

Activity 23:   The Power of Attitude   105

Activity 24:   Things That Don't Change   110

Activity 25:   Physical Exercise   116

Activity 26:   Peaceful Movement   120

Activity 27:   Breathwork   124

Activity 28:   Communicating with Your Parents   129

Activity 29:   Helping Yourself   135

Activity 30:   Getting Help from a Counselor   139

Activity 31:   Group Support   144

Activity 32:   Getting Help from Adults You Trust   149

Activity 33:   Your Right to Love Both Parents   155

Activity 34:   Your Right to Remain Separate from Parental Problems   160

Activity 35:   Your Right to Remain a Teen   165

Activity 36:   Your Right to Be Parented   169

Activity 37:   Your Right to Stay in Contact with Extended Family   173

Activity 38:   Your Right to Separate from Your Family   176

Activity 39:   If One Parent Is Far Away   180

Activity 40:   If One Parent Leaves You   186

Activity 41:   When a Parent Needs Help   190

Activity 42:   Possible Positives   194

Dear Reader,

Even though you are a teenager, you may feel like a little kid at times as you go through the experience of your parents' divorce. Having a family split apart is a challenging and life-changing situation that can make anyone feel shaky and insecure. You are facing a change that you probably didn't want or ask for. It is normal to be upset, but you can meet and conquer this challenge.

This book is designed specifically to help you work through and successfully handle the experience of your parents' divorce. The exercises presented here won't magically make things better. They won't prevent your parents from splitting up, and they won't get them back together again. What they will do is help you better understand your thoughts and feelings about the situation, and provide you with coping skills to handle it.

There are some aspects of divorce that are the same across the board, and others will vary from family to family. As you read through this book, you will learn about other teens' experiences of divorce. Some will be similar to your own, and some will be very different. Not all of the exercises here will be relevant for you. Feel free to take what helps you most from each activity and leave what doesn't apply.

As you work through these exercises, and through the process of change, be patient and gentle with yourself—and don't give up. Many other teens have gone through similar times and have come out on the other side. Try to strike a balance between facing your feelings and taking a break from them. Both behaviors are necessary in order to grow and heal.

Many teens find the experience of divorce easier to handle when they have someone to share it with. Don't hesitate to find a friend, counselor, or other adult to talk to about the exercises in this book. And know that the more you do to help yourself, the easier it will be to manage this life event.

Good luck to you, and congratulations on taking a wise and mature step toward self-help.

Lisa M. Schab

your thoughts and feelings 1

for you to know

When parents decide to divorce, it is rare that anyone can change their minds, not even their own children. It might feel like your parents are making this decision without considering you at all. Expressing your thoughts and feelings can help you realize their validity.

Bryan was shocked when his parents told him they were getting divorced. He knew they argued a lot, but they had argued since he was very young; he never thought they would actually split up. Bryan's brother, Brad, was away at college. Bryan talked to Brad about the divorce a few times, but not to anyone else.

Eventually, Bryan felt himself getting angry. He was snapping at his girlfriend, he was short with his teachers and coach, and he was driving more aggressively than he used to. The divorce was on his mind all the time. He tried to talk to his mom and asked her if there were any chance they would change their minds. His mom just gave him a stern look and said no.

Bryan was supposed to write an English paper on something he felt strongly about. He had planned to write about the dangers of smoking, because his uncle had died from lung cancer. But when he sat down at the computer, his mind kept wandering to the divorce, and he found himself writing about that instead. He wrote what he thought and felt about his parents' decision to end their marriage. When he read the paper out loud in class, he realized that it felt good to express his opinion and also to have someone listen to his side of things.

for you to do

Pretend you have to give a speech telling both the negative and positive aspects of divorce. In preparation for your speech, write a list of the pros and cons here. Number your points in order of importance.

	Pros of Divorce	Cons of Divorce
◯		
◯		
◯		

Now write a very brief introduction to your speech. What would you say to catch the audience's attention?

	Introduction
○	
○	

Tell how your personal experience with divorce affects how you feel about it as a life choice.

_____

_____

_____

_____

_____

...and more to do!

Tell why you do or do not feel that your parents listened to your feelings about their getting divorced.

_____

_____

Tell what you think about your parents' decision to divorce. (Remember that thoughts are different from feelings.)

_____

_____

Do you think your parents will be happier living apart? _____

Do you think that they could have worked out their differences if they had tried harder? Why or why not?

_____

_____

If your parents had asked for your opinion before they made their decision, what would you have told them?

_____

Tell how you feel about your parents' decision to divorce. (Remember that feelings are different from thoughts.)

_____

_____

On a separate piece of paper, write a letter to your parents, telling them what you think and feel about their decision to divorce. (This is not a letter that you have to send. Talk with a counselor about whether it would be a good idea to share these thoughts and feelings with your parents.)

for you to know

Going through the experience of their parents' divorce is a challenge for any teen. It is a time of high emotion and a time of change. While it may be one of the hardest things you ever do, it is possible to make it more manageable by doing two important things: expressing your thoughts and feelings and finding people to help you.

Mariah didn't want anyone to know about her parents' divorce. She didn't want to talk about it and she didn't want to think about it. She didn't even want to say the word out loud. She hoped her parents would change their minds. She hoped that in a few days or weeks they would come to her and say, "Guess what! We've changed our minds. We're going to stay together."

A month went by but nothing changed, except that Mariah was getting headaches almost every day. The doctor could find nothing physically wrong and asked if Mariah was under any kind of stress. Mariah said no, that nothing was wrong. Then the doctor asked how she felt about her parents' divorce. Mariah was taken by surprise and tears came to her eyes. She said that she didn't want to talk about it, but she couldn't seem to stop her tears.

Mariah's doctor said that he wouldn't force her to talk about it with him, but he thought it was important that she share her feelings with someone. He said that he thought her headaches might be coming from all the tension she was holding inside.

That night, Mariah went to her aunt and uncle's house. She had felt close to them since she was a little girl. For the first time in weeks, she opened up and talked about how she felt. She told them how upset she was, how angry at her parents, and how scared that she'd have to move and change schools. When she was done, she felt tired, but also relaxed. The next day she had no headache.

As time went on, Mariah continued to talk with her aunt and uncle. She never stopped disliking the fact that her parents were splitting up, but her headaches went away and she didn't feel as sad.

for you to do

In the box below, draw an outline of your body. Inside your body space, write the names of feelings that you might be holding in. Outside your body space, write the names of feelings that you have expressed.

Tell what you think about the idea that holding in painful feelings can cause physical pain.

_____

_____

_____

_____

_____

_____

_____

Describe any time in your life when you might have experienced physical pain that was caused by holding in feelings.

_____

_____

_____

_____

_____

_____

_____

...and more to do!

Why do you think Mariah didn't want to think or talk about her parents' divorce?

_____

_____

_____

_____

Why do you think Mariah talked to her aunt and uncle instead of her doctor?

_____

_____

_____

_____

Tell what you think Mariah might have said to her aunt and uncle.

_____

_____

_____

_____

Next to each of the words below, write the name of a specific person in your life who might be able to listen to you or help you express your feelings about your parents' divorce.

Teacher _____   Uncle _____

Counselor _____   Other family member _____

Friend _____   Neighbor _____

Coach _____   Spiritual leader _____

Grandparent _____   School employee _____

Aunt _____   Other adult _____

If you are feeling upset about the divorce, make a plan to talk with one of these people in the next week. Tell when and where you will meet.

_____

_____

_____

Explain what you would like to tell this person.

_____

_____

_____

_____

3 acting out

for you to know

When people experience very strong feelings but don't recognize them or manage them in a healthy way, those feelings can come out though negative behavior. This is called "acting out" feelings. Negative behaviors may include aggression towards self or others, delinquency, substance use, or sexual promiscuity. You can keep yourself from acting out by addressing and expressing your feelings directly.

Jeremy had never been in trouble at school before, but since his father had moved out, he found himself in the assistant principal's office three weeks in a row. The first week, another student had been making fun of him, and Jeremy had pushed him into a locker so hard that it cut his arm. The second week, Jeremy had been sent to the office for swearing at his history teacher. The third week, Jeremy had been found responsible for lighting firecrackers; two other students had been injured.

Andrea told everyone she didn't care about her parents divorcing. She said that she was going to move out as soon as she turned eighteen anyway, so it didn't really matter. She rarely saw her mother anymore now that her mom had gone back to work full-time. Her dad had cancelled more than half his custody visits, but Andrea said she didn't care about that either because it gave her more time to be with her friends. One day Andrea's mother got a call that Andrea had been caught shoplifting, even though she'd had plenty of money with her.

When Chris's mom told him she was leaving his father and marrying someone else, Chris knew he had never felt so depressed in his life. At first he thought it wouldn't really happen, but when she packed her suitcase and moved out, he knew it was real. He started to hang out with different kids. Although he had always thought drugs and alcohol were for losers, he began to smoke marijuana and take some of his dad's beer to share with other kids when he went to parties. One night a party got busted, and Chris ended up at the police station.

Neither Jeremy nor Andrea nor Chris had intended to do anything that would get them into trouble, but it happened nonetheless. None of them were aware of how their behaviors were connected to their feelings about their parents' divorces.

for you to do

Read the previous stories again. Try to put yourself in the position of each of these teens and think about what it would be like to be in their shoes. Then answer the questions below.

What might Jeremy have been feeling about his father moving out?

_____

_____

_____

Do you think Jeremy wanted to get into trouble at school? Why or why not?

_____

_____

_____

How could Jeremy's feelings about his parents' divorce be connected to his negative behaviors?

_____

_____

_____

Do you think Andrea really cared about her parents' divorce? Explain your answer.

_____

_____

_____

How do you think Andrea felt about her parents having much less time for her?

_____

_____

What reason would Andrea have for shoplifting if she could afford to pay for her items?

_____

_____

Describe what thoughts and feelings you think Chris might have had when he heard that his mother was divorcing his father and marrying someone else.

_____

_____

_____

Why do you think Chris would start using drugs and alcohol when he had never wanted to before?

_____

_____

_____

How could these teens have expressed their feelings directly and in a more appropriate way than acting them out?

_____

_____

_____

...and more to do!

Think about your own behavior since you learned about your parents' divorce. Circle any of the phrases below that describe things you have done to act out your feelings.

stopped doing homework	used excessive profanity	used alcohol
broke the law	used drugs	stopped studying
skipped classes	became argumentative	stopped eating
was sexually promiscuous	started lying	stopped bathing
was physically harmful to others	ran away from home	drove dangerously
was physically harmful to self	vandalized property	broke curfew

Describe any other behaviors you have performed that might represent acting out your feelings.

_____

_____

Make a list of the feelings that might be underlying your acting-out behavior.

_____

_____

Tell what the negative consequences of your acting-out behaviors have been, or could be.

_____

_____

Describe any ways you can think of right now to express your feelings more appropriately than acting them out with negative behaviors.

_____

_____

4 guilt

When David and Amy's parents got divorced, the two siblings talked about what they could have done to keep the divorce from happening. They talked about how often the two of them had argued about who would use the bathroom first or whose turn it was to empty the dishwasher or feed the dog. Their parents would get upset with them at these times and then usually got upset with each other as well. David and Amy thought maybe if they had gotten along better, their parents' marriage could have been saved.

David also wondered if his football injury had something to do with it. The year he had dislocated his knee, there had been many doctor and hospital bills and bills for physical therapy. David knew his parents fought over money a lot, and he wondered if all of his medical bills had put them over the edge.

Amy thought about her trouble in reading. She had often needed tutoring, and she always felt like she'd failed her parents. Sometimes they had to spend a lot of time giving her extra help with her homework. She thought that maybe if she'd been a better student they wouldn't have had to worry about her and could have had a better marriage.

One weekend when David and Amy were visiting their dad, he heard them talking about this. He sat down with them and explained in no uncertain terms that the divorce had had nothing to do with them. It was about his and their mother's inability to get along, and that was no one else's fault. He even got their mother on the phone to confirm it, and she agreed. The divorce definitely did not happen because of anything David or Amy had ever done or not done. There was absolutely nothing for them to feel guilty about.

for you to do

Guilt is a feeling we experience when we tell ourselves that we are responsible for doing something that we judge as wrong or negative. Below each picture, explain what you think the teen is feeling guilty about.

_____

_____

_____

_____

_____

_____

activity 4 ✳ guilt

Did the teens in these pictures actually do something wrong?

_____

_____

Explain how the situations above are different from the thought of feeling guilty for your parents getting divorced.

_____

_____

_____

_____

_____

_____

_____

...and more to do!

Did you ever think that you might have done something to cause your parents' divorce? Explain here.

_____

_____

_____

Do you understand that divorce is not caused by kids, teens, or anyone but the two people who are getting divorced? Explain your answer.

_____

_____

Write down any other questions, thoughts, or feelings that you might have about this.

_____

_____

_____

If you have any feelings of guilt about your parents' divorce, plan to talk to them or someone else about it. Explain who you could talk to and what you would like to say.

_____

_____

Make a plan to talk to someone about your feelings and follow through with it. Describe what happened when you did talk with them.

_____

_____

5 fear

Nathan couldn't believe that he was feeling nervous. He prided himself on being an independent person and pretty mature for his age. He was the one his friends came to for advice. But his parents' divorce was throwing him off balance. Every time he thought about it, he started to feel a little queasy and even light-headed sometimes. He had learned in health class that these were classic signs of anxiety or panic, and he was mad at himself for having these reactions; he thought they were wimpy.

He tried to ignore his uncomfortable feelings, but as the day of his parents' separation drew closer, his symptoms became worse. One day in computer class, the teacher asked if he'd like to go to the nurse's office—she thought he looked pale and somewhat weak. Nathan was embarrassed, but he did go to see the nurse and ended up having a long talk with her. The nurse couldn't find anything physically wrong with Nathan, but she said that his symptoms could be due to anxiety, and asked if he was under any stress. Nathan ended up telling her about his family situation, and later decided that talking with her was the best thing he'd ever done. The nurse pulled a piece of paper out of her file drawer and went over it with him. It described three steps to help him to deal with his fears: collecting information, assessing possibilities, and using strengths. That night at home, Nathan started practicing these steps, and within a couple of weeks his nausea and dizziness had disappeared.

for you to do

The following list describes some common fears that many teens experience when their parents get divorced. Put a check mark next to any fears that you have experienced yourself.

- ☐ Never seeing one parent again
- ☐ Moving to a new home
- ☐ Losing friends
- ☐ Changing schools
- ☐ Being put in the middle of parents' arguments
- ☐ Being blamed for the divorce
- ☐ Being gossiped about
- ☐ Not having enough money
- ☐ Losing a sense of family
- ☐ Losing family traditions
- ☐ A parent remarrying
- ☐ Having a stepfamily
- ☐ Losing closeness with one parent
- ☐ Being asked to take sides
- ☐ Having to fill the absent parent's shoes
- ☐ Having to care for a hurting parent
- ☐ Not being able to succeed at marriage yourself
- ☐ One or both parents won't be able to care for you

Describe any other fears you have that aren't listed above.

_____

_____

Look at the fears you have checked. Rewrite them below, putting them in order of greatest fear to smallest fear.

_____   _____

_____   _____

_____   _____

_____   _____

_____   _____

_____   _____

_____   _____

_____   _____

Make a list of other things that have happened over the course of your life that you have felt afraid of.

_____

_____

_____

_____

Describe what you did to get past your fears in these other situations. You may have to think about this for a while if you are not used to this type of self-reflection.

_____

_____

_____

_____

...and more to do!

The nurse's handout described the following ideas for dealing with fear, apprehension, and anxiety:

Dealing with Fear, Apprehension, and Anxiety

1. Collect information

Many times we are afraid of things that are unknown. Gathering as much information as possible can help us feel more confident. For example, if you are afraid that when your parents divorce you might never see one parent again, collect information by talking to your parents: Ask what the visitation schedule will be; find out how you will get from one parent's house to the other; ask if you will ever be able to see your noncustodial parent on an extra day even if it's not a scheduled visitation; find out if you can celebrate holidays with both parents. Ask questions about any fears you have.

2. Assess possibilities

This step involves checking out the chances of your fears actually coming true. Our fears are often based on worst-case scenarios, and when we think rationally, we know that the worst usually doesn't happen. Once you determine the real possibility of your fear coming true, then think about what you would do if it did happen. How would you cope? What actions could you take to care for yourself? What actions could you take to seek help from others? For example, if you are afraid that your custodial parent might run out of money, talk to your parents about their financial plan. Ask them what the chances are that there will not be enough money to pay for your food, clothing, and shelter. If they say that there is a very high chance that this will happen, find out what steps will be taken next. Will one parent take a second job? Will you have to work to contribute to the household? Are there relatives who could help out? Usually the worst does not happen, but if it does, know that there is a plan of action to get you through.

---

3. Use your strengths

No one likes to think about their fears coming true, but we feel more afraid if we believe we can't handle what will happen. When we stop to think about it, we usually find that we have strengths that help us to manage hard situations—and that includes facing our fears. Our strengths are emotional, mental, physical, or spiritual qualities that help us to either cope with or improve a situation. For example, if you are afraid of moving and starting a new school, think about your strengths and how using them can help you manage this challenge. You can remember how you started a new school when you moved from grade school to middle school, and you survived. You might think about how people tell you that you are good at taking pictures, and you could join the new school's camera club or yearbook staff to meet new friends. You might draw on your belief that there is some good in every situation and consciously look for positive things that will come from this move. Recognizing and using your strengths can help you cope with your fears.

Describe in more detail one of your fears about your parents getting divorced.

_____

_____

_____

Describe how you might use each of these coping skills to manage your fear. You can look back at what you wrote earlier in this exercise about how you handled previous fears in your life to help you answer this.

What information I will collect: _____

_____

What possibilities I will assess: _____

_____

What strengths I will use: _____

_____

sadness and depression 6

for you to know

Teens often experience sadness or depression when their parents divorce. Depression is a deeper, more pervasive type of sadness. You can help yourself manage these feelings by being aware of them, expressing them, taking action to find relief, and getting help if necessary.

Alicia and Brandy were in a support group for teens whose parents were going through a divorce. At the meetings, members would share their feelings and listen to other people's stories. Alicia and Brandy discovered that they both suffered most from feeling sad about what was happening, but they were experiencing different levels of sadness.

Alicia sometimes found herself crying when she was alone and started thinking about the divorce. She couldn't always concentrate in school and didn't feel like going out with her friends as much. She found that if she encouraged herself to keep going, she could get involved with something that took her mind off the divorce, like her work as a hospital volunteer, and she would feel better after a while.

Brandy's sadness interfered in her daily life. Often she didn't want to get out of bed in the morning. She missed her bus and then would skip school. In the evenings she just lay on the couch and watched TV. She lost her appetite and stopped going to her dance lessons. Her grades were falling and she always felt tired.

The support group leader, Mr. Sommers, helped both girls. He encouraged Alicia to continue expressing her feelings during the group and to keep a journal of her feelings. He thought it was a good idea for her to continue going out with her friends and also to spend more time with her volunteer work because helping other people took her mind off her own problems.

He met with Brandy and her parents and recommended that Brandy get some help. He told her parents it was important that she begin eating well again and attending school regularly. He gave them the name of a counselor whom Brandy could talk with at weekly sessions in addition to the support group. All of this helped, and eventually Brandy started to feel better.

for you to do

Rate yourself on the scales below according to how much you are experiencing these symptoms of sadness.

	not at all				moderately				extremely	
Crying	1	2	3	4	5	6	7	8	9	10
Not eating well	1	2	3	4	5	6	7	8	9	10
Not sleeping well	1	2	3	4	5	6	7	8	9	10
Feeling down	1	2	3	4	5	6	7	8	9	10
Feeling tired	1	2	3	4	5	6	7	8	9	10
Not wanting to be with friends	1	2	3	4	5	6	7	8	9	10
Feeling discouraged about the future	1	2	3	4	5	6	7	8	9	10
Declining interest in previously enjoyed activities	1	2	3	4	5	6	7	8	9	10
Dropping grades	1	2	3	4	5	6	7	8	9	10
Getting into trouble	1	2	3	4	5	6	7	8	9	10
Feeling helpless	1	2	3	4	5	6	7	8	9	10
Having a hard time concentrating	1	2	3	4	5	6	7	8	9	10
Feeling worthless	1	2	3	4	5	6	7	8	9	10
Feeling guilty	1	2	3	4	5	6	7	8	9	10

Look back at your ratings. How many symptoms did you rate at a number higher than 5?

_____

Do you think sadness is interfering with your relationships? Explain why or why not.

_____

_____

_____

Are your feelings of sadness keeping you from going to school or maintaining your grades? Explain why or why not.

_____

_____

_____

_____

Describe your feelings of sadness here, and tell what you feel the saddest about and why.

_____

_____

_____

_____

_____

Share your ratings and answers with your parent, counselor, or other adult whom you trust. Talk about how deep your sadness is, and whether you should get some extra help to deal with it.

...and more to do!

The previous exercises in this activity should have helped you be aware of your feelings. Expressing your feelings is an important step towards feeling better. The phrases below describe ways to safely express sadness. Circle any of them that you already do.

cry	talk to a friend	write in a journal
play music	draw or paint	talk to a counselor
go for a walk	pet an animal	practice yoga
talk to a relative	practice deep breathing	write poetry

Describe any other ways that you express sadness.

_____

_____

_____

Which of the above activities appeal to you as ways to express sadness?

_____

_____

Along with acknowledging sadness and letting it out, it is important to take a break from thinking about it. Tell what activities you like to do that take your mind off of sadness and help you feel happy.

_____

_____

Which of these activities can you plan to do within the next few days? Be sure to carry out your plan.

_____

_____

_____

_____

If you are recognizing, expressing, and taking breaks from your sadness, but these steps are not helping enough, or if your sadness feels very deep and is interfering in your life, it is important for you to find some extra help. Talk to your parent, or counselor, or other adult who can help you with this. Show them this exercise, or explain to them the depth of your sadness. If you don't feel there is anyone to help you, you can call for help by dialing 911 on your phone, or calling or going to a local hospital emergency room.

7 anger

Ian was very angry about his parents' divorce. He could barely look at them without feeling his anger well up inside. He knew he would get in trouble if he screamed at them, so he held in his anger. One day when his mother left for work, he went into his room, slammed the door, and put his fist through his bedroom wall.

Nikki was very angry about her parents' divorce. She could barely look at them without feeling her anger well up inside. She knew she would get in trouble if she screamed at them, so she held in her anger. At school she would pretend to be happy, and she continued to hold in her anger. She found it hard to concentrate in class and started forgetting to turn in homework. She came home at the end of each day with her upper back and shoulders aching.

Ramon was very angry about his parents' divorce. He could barely look at them without feeling his anger well up inside. He knew he would get in trouble if he screamed at them, so he held in his anger. He started getting into fights at school. Anyone who irritated him in the slightest way would get shoved or tripped. His school had a zero tolerance policy for violence, and it wasn't long before Ramon was suspended.

Each of these teens had a right to feel and express anger, but none of them handled it in a healthy or appropriate way.

for you to do

The pictures below show Ian, Nikki, and Ramon dealing with their anger.

The phrases below describe healthier and safer ways to express anger. Put an "I" by the phrases that you think might help Ian, put an "N" by the phrases that you think might help Nikki, and put an "R" by the phrases that you think might help Ramon.

talking about it	writing about it	playing music
running	shooting baskets	dancing
pounding pillows	swimming	walking briskly
bike riding	kicking a ball around	punching a punching bag
drawing it on paper	yelling alone outside	singing loudly

Add any other ideas that you have:

_____

_____

_____

...and more to do!

Make a list of things that you are angry about regarding your parents' divorce.
Number them in order from those that make you feel the most angry to those that
make you the least angry.

_____	_____
_____	_____
_____	_____
_____	_____

In the box below, draw a stick figure or simple shape that represents you. Then using
lines, shapes, or shading, show your anger and where it exists, within or around you.
Try to show how big and how strong it feels.

Describe how you usually let out your feelings of anger.

_____

_____

_____

Tell which of the actions you take are safe and appropriate ways to express anger and which are not safe or appropriate.

_____

_____

_____

_____

Look again at the list of phrases. Tell which ones you think could help you.

_____

_____

_____

Talk with a counselor or other adult about how you can actually put these ideas into practice. The next time you feel angry, try to express it safely. Describe what happens.

_____

_____

_____

_____

_____

8 grief and loss

for you to know

When things change in our lives, something is always lost. When your parents divorce, your family changes. Even if you still see both of them and know that they both love you, the way that your family once existed is lost. It is normal to feel grief when you experience loss.

Elisabeth Kubler-Ross, M.D. was the first to identify the now well-known five stages of grieving that humans pass through when they experience a loss. These stages can be applied to the loss that comes with divorce. It is important to note that movement through the five stages is not linear. You won't experience one stage, complete it, and then move on to the next. You may pass through the stages in any order and may revisit one or more of them more than once.

1. **Denial:** You can't believe it is true that your parents are getting divorced. You try to deny that it is happening, or your mind does not let you believe that it could happen. You may think, "This can't be real."

2. **Anger:** You feel angry that your parents are getting divorced. You don't want it to happen, and you are mad at them or their marriage counselor or your grandparents or the world for allowing it to happen.

3. **Bargaining:** Maybe you try to talk your parents out of the divorce. You might tell them that you'll get straight A's this semester if they don't get divorced. You might say that you'll never fight with your sister again if they don't get divorced. Maybe you try to bargain with God: You try to make a deal that if your parents stay together you'll never be sarcastic again, or you'll donate half your allowance to needy kids.

4. **Depression:** You start to feel a sense of loss and sadness at what is happening to you and your family. You think about all the changes that you do not want and will not like. You might feel hopeless or helpless. You feel very downhearted.

5. **Acceptance:** In this stage, you finally stop fighting the fact of the divorce and begin to come to terms with what is happening.

for you to do

In the box below, draw a sketch of the way your family lived before your parents were divorced. Show where you lived and who lived together. Show how people were emotionally connected.

In this box, draw a sketch of your family after the divorce. Show the changes in where you live and who lives together. Show how people are now emotionally connected.

Tell what it feels like to look at this visual representation of the change in your family.

_____

_____

_____

_____

_____

_____

_____

Describe what you have lost by your parents getting divorced.

_____

_____

_____

_____

_____

_____

_____

_____

...and more to do!

Tell whether and how you have experienced each of these stages of grieving.

Denial _____

_____

Anger _____

_____

Bargaining _____

_____

Depression _____

_____

Acceptance _____

_____

Everyone experiences grief differently. It is normal for grief to come and go; one day you might think it's all gone, and the next day you feel bad again. The following ideas have helped people cope with grief. Put a check mark next to any that you think might help you.

☐ Express your feelings. Talk or write about your grief in a way that feels safe to you.

☐ Develop a support network. Make a list of people you feel comfortable going to when you feel like you need company.

☐ Take your mind off your grief. Listen to music, go to a movie, play a sport, or go out with friends.

☐ Think about what you still have. You may have suffered some losses because of your parents' divorce, but there are also many things you haven't lost: your health, your education, your talents and skills, your friends, your parents' love.

☐ Focus on what you can control. You couldn't keep your parents from getting divorced, but there are many things you do have control of: who you choose for friends, what activities you participate in, what you want to do with your future, what kind of a person you want to be.

☐ Take care of yourself. Feelings of grief can be physically draining. Getting enough sleep and exercise, and eating well can help keep you feeling strong and healthy.

☐ Avoid addictive activities. Alcohol, drugs, and food may provide a temporary escape from your feelings, but they can also become addictive, and addictions do not allow you to heal.

Give yourself time to heal. Be patient with yourself. Divorce creates a big change in your life. Allow yourself time to adjust.

Describe how you can put any of these ideas into action.

_____

_____

_____

_____

_____

_____

_____

abandonment 9

Lyndsay sat by herself on the bleachers wondering what to do. She wanted to go with her friends on their school's weekend ski trip, but at the same time, she didn't want to leave home. She knew she would have fun if she went, but she also felt a little nervous. Thinking about her parents splitting up made her feel like she was standing in shifting sand; she didn't have the secure feeling that she used to have.

The ski club sponsor was Mr. Davis, her social studies teacher. When he saw that Lyndsay hadn't turned in her registration for the trip, he asked her why she was hesitating. Lyndsay said she wasn't sure. She explained that ever since she found out her parents were getting divorced, she felt almost like a little kid who was lost in the supermarket and couldn't find her mom. She felt like her parents were leaving her right at a time when she needed them to be there so she could leave them.

Lyndsay wasn't sure if what she said made any sense, but Mr. Davis seemed to understand. He said that his parents had gotten divorced when he was fifteen, and he also had felt a sense of abandonment. He said that there were a few things Lyndsay could do to help herself feel better. He wrote these ideas down on a piece of paper, and suggested that she try any or all of them, and then let him know how they worked.

Here is what he wrote:

○ 1. Tell your mom and dad how you feel. Let them reassure you that they love you and will still be your parents even if they are divorced. Make sure you spend regular time with each of them.

2. Stay close to your extended family; your sense of security can be bolstered by your connection to them as well. Visit or talk to your grandparents, aunts, uncles, and cousins. Keep celebrating holidays with them.

○ 3. Stay in touch with other adults to whom you feel close: a teacher, counselor, coach, neighbor, spiritual leader, or someone else. Remember that they are there to support you when you need them.

4. Continue to go out with your friends and participate in safe activities that you enjoy. When you try new things, have fun, and have successes, you will build confidence in yourself.

○ 5. Remember that your parents were together for many years and were with you during your formative years. The ideals and love they instilled in you are still there. Continue to hold on to their wisdom and love that you carry within you.

for you to do

In each of the pictures below, describe what you think is happening and how the teen is feeling.

_____   _____

_____   _____

_____   _____

_____   _____

_____   _____

Draw two similar pictures depicting yourself and details from your own life.

Describe what you are thinking and feeling in each of your pictures.

_____   _____

_____   _____

_____   _____

_____   _____

_____   _____

_____   _____

…and more to do!

Think about the list of ideas that Mr. Davis gave Lyndsay, and answer these questions.

Do you believe that your parents still love you even if they are divorced? Describe what they say or do that proves this to you.

_____

_____

_____

If you don't believe it, plan a time to talk with your parents. You can show them this exercise if it will help you bring up the subject.

Are you able to spend as much time as you need with each of your parents? If not, talk to them about how this can be improved.

List the people in your extended family that you feel close to. How can you plan to continue seeing them on a regular basis?

_____	_____
_____	_____
_____	_____
_____	_____

If you are afraid you won't be able to stay connected to them, talk to your parents—or your extended family members—about how you can make this happen.

List other adults whom you feel close to. Number them in order of whom you might turn to first, second, third, and so on.

_____   _____

_____   _____

_____   _____

List any activities you are interested in becoming involved in, or areas that you are interested in pursuing, to help you develop as a unique individual. Next to each one, tell what you could specifically do to take a step toward it.

_____   _____

_____   _____

_____   _____

_____   _____

Plan to take one of these steps in the next two weeks. After you have done it, describe your experience here.

_____

_____

_____

Make a list of things your parents have taught you or instilled in you that you value and will carry into adulthood.

_____

_____

_____

_____

neglect 10

for you to know

When parents get divorced, they are making a significant change in their lives that takes up a lot of time, as well as physical and emotional energy. Divorce may require them to work more hours at their jobs, meet with lawyers and counselors, or make plans for moving. Because parents are paying so much attention to themselves during this period, teens can often feel neglected.

Michael fixed himself dinner in the microwave and sat down to watch TV. He felt awful. He was tired of coming home to an empty house. He was tired of heating up dinners. He was tired of everything in his family's life revolving around the stupid divorce.

It seemed like all his parents talked about anymore was the divorce. "Things are going to change, Michael—you're going to have to be more independent." "I won't be home to make you dinner, honey. We've got a meeting with the lawyer." "I can't make it to your game this weekend, Michael. I've got to look at an apartment." Michael had hated the divorce from the beginning, and as time went on, he hated it even more. His parents used to have time for him. Even though he complained sometimes, he had liked having dinner as a family or going to Aunt Mary's for Sunday Scrabble games. He had liked it when his mom had time to fold his laundry and his dad helped him with his algebra. Now they were almost never home, or if they were, they were fighting about who would get the piano or the bedroom furniture.

One night while he was studying at his friend Erik's house, he e-mailed his parents. He stretched the truth a little because he was angry. He wrote: "Hi, remember me? I won't be coming home for a while. Not that you'll notice. Michael." Then he made plans to spend the night at Erik's house and go to school from there the next day. When Michael's mom read the e-mail later that night, she called his father and they both went to Erik's house to bring Michael home. Then the three of them sat down and talked. They told Michael it was important that he talk to them about his feelings, rather than getting mad and staying away. Michael didn't want to say anything at first, but finally he told them how neglected he felt, like he didn't have parents anymore. His parents said that it was hard on them, too, but they apologized for not being there for him. They set a goal to spend more time together and wrote down specific ways to achieve it. Things never went completely back to normal, because his parents still got divorced. But they did work at achieving their goal, and that made Michael feel better.

for you to do

This is a copy of Michael's e-mail message to his parents.

Subject: Hi from your son

From: michael@qxy.com

Date: May 10 9:30 p.m.

To: momndad@qxy.com

Message:

Hi, remember me? I won't be coming home for a while. Not that you'll notice.

Michael

Tell what you think Michael was feeling that would have made him say these things.

_____

_____

Michael used a lot of sarcasm in his e-mail. Rewrite his message below in an honest and straightforward way and without using sarcasm.

Subject: Hi from your son

From: michael@qxy.com

Date: May 10 9:30 p.m.

To: momndad@qxy.com

Message:

_____

_____

What message do you think Michael was trying to convey in his first e-mail?

_____

_____

...and more to do!

When parents are divorcing, their time can be taken up in any or all of the following ways. Circle any of the phrases below that describe your parents.

talking on the phone more to friends	complaining about legal fees
spending more time at work	arguing with each other
looking for new jobs	looking for new places to live
going to meetings with lawyers	crying or being sad
staring off into space	sleeping more
not listening to what you are saying	forgetting responsibilities
using alcohol or drugs	going to counselors
complaining about each other	going out with friends more
watching more TV	talking about financial worries

Describe anything else your parents do because of the divorce that gives them less time to pay attention to you.

_____

_____

_____

Have you ever felt neglected? Explain how your feelings were similar to or different from Michael's.

_____

_____

_____

_____

If you feel neglected, you can help yourself by:

1. Telling your parents how you feel and asking what they could realistically do to change this.

2. Keeping yourself busy with safe activities that you enjoy—being with friends, participating in sports or other school clubs or activities, etc.

3. Talking to someone about your feelings—a relative, friend, teacher, counselor, or someone else whom you trust.

11 happiness

for you to know

While many of the emotions associated with divorce feel bad to us, it can also be normal to feel something good. Sometimes teens feel relieved, or even happy, when their parents get divorced. If they don't understand that this feeling is normal, they can feel guilty about their happiness.

Jessie's parents had been going through their divorce process for almost four years. Because they had a lot of property and possessions, because they had four children over a spread of ages, and because they were very bitter and had a hard time agreeing on the divorce terms, the process dragged on and on.

Jessie, age thirteen, was the oldest of the siblings. Her sister was ten, and her two brothers were seven and five. All of them had watched their parents argue about the divorce for four years. They all disliked the disagreements, and they disliked that their father sometimes stayed with them and sometimes lived in another house. They thought their mom might have a boyfriend, and they disliked that, too. They didn't feel like they were a "married" family and they didn't feel like they were a "divorced" family. Being somewhere in the middle felt upsetting and confusing.

When the day came that the divorce was final, Jessie couldn't believe how happy she felt. It was finally over! But as soon as she felt this surge of happiness, she began to cry. She felt ashamed and guilty and scared. She thought there must be something very wrong with her if she was happy that her parents were divorced. The next day she talked to her counselor, who said that it was perfectly normal for Jessie to feel this way, considering all the difficulties she had been through for the past few years. She said that Jessie might feel relieved that it was over and they could get on with their lives in a more peaceful manner.

for you to do

There are many valid reasons why teens might feel happy when their parents get divorced. But sometimes kids also pretend to be happy about it just to cover up their real feelings. Put an "R" next to the statements that you think describe real feelings of happiness, and put a "CU" next to the statements that you think represent a cover-up for other feelings.

"It was actually nice when my parents started living separately because I didn't have to lie awake at night and listen to them argue anymore."

"When my parents got divorced and I had to go to my dad's house on weekends, I found myself having more time with him than when he'd lived at our house. I realized that I liked this change."

"I'm glad my parents got divorced. Now there's only one person to nag me."

"Sometimes I am actually happy that my parents got divorced. Now my mom is so much more relaxed and even fun to be with. The divorce has made a really good change in her."

"My parents get along better now that they're divorced. That's something I'm actually happy about."

"It's cool that my parents got divorced. It's their life; it really doesn't affect me anyway."

"It's good that my parents got divorced. My dad is a real loser. My mom is better off without him."

If you put a CU next to any of the preceding statements, explain what feelings you think these teens were trying to cover up.

_____

_____

_____

_____

_____

_____

_____

_____

_____

...and more to do!

If you have ever really felt happy about your parents' divorce, explain your reasons here.

_____

_____

If you have ever pretended to be happy about your parents' divorce, explain your reasons here.

_____

_____

Tell whether you think Jessie was truly happy about her parents' divorce, and explain your answer.

_____

_____

_____

It is important to know that even if you have reasons to feel happy about your parents' divorce, you can still have reasons to feel unhappy about it as well. It is rarely an all-or-nothing situation. On the scales below, record approximately what percentage of your feelings about your parents' divorce are happy and what percentage are unhappy.

Percentage That I Am Happy

| 0% | 10% | 20% | 30% | 40% | 50% | 60% | 70% | 80% | 90% | 100% |

Percentage That I Am Unhappy

| 0% | 10% | 20% | 30% | 40% | 50% | 60% | 70% | 80% | 90% | 100% |

12 confusion

for you to know

It is normal to feel many different feelings simultaneously when your parents get divorced. You may feel a combination of sadness, fear, happiness, guilt, anger, or other feelings. You may have many conflicting thoughts. These feelings can cause you to feel confused, which is a normal reaction to the situation.

Curtis thought he knew what he wanted in life. He knew he wanted to be an engineer like his dad; he knew he wanted to live in the city; he knew he wanted to travel to lots of cool places; he knew he wanted to have a wife and kids someday. He thought he knew himself pretty well, too. He knew he liked basketball; he knew he liked science a lot and English very little; he knew he liked girls with a sense of humor; he knew he might drink beer but would never do drugs; he knew he believed that hard work got people far in life.

But when Curtis's parents got divorced, it seemed like everything changed. All of a sudden, he didn't feel as sure of anything. He was mad at his dad and didn't know if he still wanted to be an engineer, much less like him in any way. He thought he might never want to get married if it could end in the pain of divorce. He wasn't sure that life was fair anymore, and wondered if all the hard work he did at school was really worth it. Curtis felt so confused, like a rug had been pulled out from under him.

In an argument Curtis told his dad that he hated him. They were both taken aback, but his dad could tell that Curtis was very upset. He let Curtis calm down, and then they talked. Curtis told his dad about all the confusing feelings and thoughts he had been having. His dad told him that the thoughts and feelings were normal—everyone in the family was having them. There was a huge change in their lives. They had all lost something that they believed in, and it was hard to find a peaceful way to think about it.

The next weekend, Curtis and his brothers and his dad talked more about the way the divorce was affecting their lives. They shared their feelings and thoughts. Curtis was relieved to find out his older brother was confused, too. Curtis's dad said they would feel better if they identified what was making them confused, talked about these things, and realized that their feelings were normal. Curtis said he felt better already, just knowing he wasn't the only one feeling confused.

for you to do

The picture below shows Curtis surrounded by all the thoughts and feelings that are confusing him. In the next box, draw a picture of yourself, and write in anything and everything that might feel confusing to you since, or because of, your parents' divorce.

Describe how your picture is similar to or different from Curtis's picture.

_____

_____

_____

_____

Tell what stands out to you as you look at your picture.

_____

_____

_____

_____

Tell how you feel as you look at your picture.

_____

_____

_____

_____

...and more to do!

List the confusing thoughts and feelings that you wrote in your picture.

_____

_____

_____

Which of the items on your list is the hardest for you to deal with? Explain why.

_____

_____

Which of the items on your list is the easiest for you to deal with? Explain why.

_____

_____

As you feel like it, write about any other items on your list that seem to need your attention. Use additional paper if necessary. This exercise may take a few days or even a few weeks to complete. Try to finish it within a month.

_____

_____

If there are any items on your list that are very upsetting to you, talk to a counselor or other adult about them. Describe how you feel after you talk to someone.

_____

_____

_____

other feelings 13

for you to know

We commonly think of the feelings of anger, sadness, guilt, and fear when parents get divorced. There are also many other normal feelings that a teen might experience. Identifying and accepting any other feelings you have can help you feel better.

"Sometimes I can't describe my feelings," Aubrey told the small group in her health class. "I know they come from my parents getting divorced, but I don't always know what they are."

Ms. Sedgewick, the health teacher, had asked students to divide into small groups and discuss the feelings they experience. Aubrey and a number of other students were having trouble naming exactly what their feelings were. Ms. Sedgewick said, "We often don't pay attention to our feelings, and we don't get a lot of education about them, so it isn't always easy to name them." To help the class, she gave them a handout of cartoon faces that expressed many different feelings.

Ms. Sedgewick wasn't surprised that much of the class was unaware of the variety of human feelings. They talked about what each feeling meant. They learned that different people might define the same feeling in different ways. They learned that all feelings are normal to experience at some time. Using the handout, Aubrey was able to decide that her hard-to-pinpoint feelings were probably disappointment, worry, and embarrassment—feelings she hadn't thought about before. It made her feel better to have a name for her feelings, and also to learn that her experience was normal.

for you to do

The faces below depict twenty different feelings. Next to as many faces as you can, write a note about a situation when you have experienced that feeling. If you don't understand what a particular feeling is, ask an adult or look it up in a dictionary.

worried

_____
_____
_____

brave

_____
_____
_____

calm

_____
_____
_____

confused

_____
_____
_____

disappointed

_____
_____
_____

embarrassed

_____
_____
_____

excited

_____
_____
_____

guilty

_____
_____
_____

happy

irritable

jealous

lonely

loving

mad

proud

sad

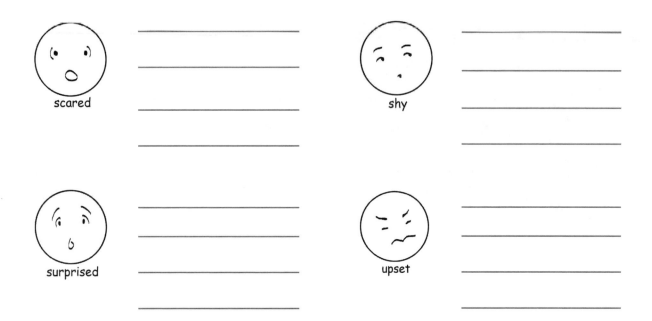

scared

shy

surprised

upset

Put a circle around the feelings you experience most often.

Put a "D" over any feeling you are experiencing in relation to your parents' divorce.

...and more to do!

Why do you think Ms. Sedgewick wanted her class to learn about feelings?

_____

_____

_____

_____

Tell why you think most people are aware of only a limited number of feelings.

_____

_____

_____

_____

List any feelings you have had related to your parents' divorce that have not been mentioned here. If you can't label your feeling, simply describe it, or describe the situation where you noticed it.

_____

_____

_____

Even if a feeling may be foreign to you, chances are there is a good reason that you are experiencing it. Remind yourself that having feelings is normal.

IMPORTANT NOTE: If you ever have a feeling that is so strong that it frightens you, tell an adult about what you are experiencing.

14 wishing for reconciliation

for you to know

Many teens of divorced parents have a dream that one day their parents will reconcile their differences and reunite. This is something that rarely happens, but it is normal to wish that it would.

One night, Danielle and her brother, Adam, were watching TV together in the family room. Out of the blue, Danielle asked Adam if he ever thought about their parents getting back together again. Adam told Danielle she was crazy—their parents had been divorced for two years and they were each dating other people, and it sure didn't look like they were going to remarry any time soon.

Danielle said she knew all that, but she still hoped it might happen someday. She thought that they might just need time to figure out that there weren't any better partners out there, and when they realized this they would reunite.

Again, Adam told Danielle she was crazy. But then a few minutes later he admitted that he did think about it sometimes. When their parents had first started divorce proceedings, Adam said he had thought about trying to keep them together. He thought maybe if he broke his leg skiing and they both had to come to the hospital to see him, they might start talking about how important their family was and decide that they really didn't want to break everyone up by getting divorced.

Danielle said she used to think that maybe if she made a really nice dinner when her mom got home from work, and put candles on the table and played soft music and called her dad to come over, her parents might have a romantic evening together and fall in love again.

Neither Adam nor Danielle had ever heard of anyone who had gotten divorced getting back together again. But Danielle said that sometimes when she was feeling anxious about something in her life, it made her feel better to think about it. Adam said it would probably never happen, but he would like it, too.

for you to do

Write your mom's name on the woman's picture on the left, and write your dad's name on the man's picture on the right. In the middle box, draw or describe any reconciliation dream you have had about your parents getting back together.

My Dream

On the scale below, circle the number that shows how much you would like this dream to really happen.

not at all   1   2   3   4   5   6   7   8   9   10   more than anything

On the scale below, circle the number that shows how realistic you think it is that this dream would really happen.

will never happen   1   2   3   4   5   6   7   8   9   10   will definitely happen

...and more to do!

Tell why you think that kids of all ages would like their divorced parents to get back together again.

_____

_____

Describe any situations you know of where divorced couples reunited.

_____

_____

_____

Explain why you think Danielle liked to dream about her parents getting back together when she was feeling anxious about something in her life.

_____

_____

How do you feel when you think about your parents getting back together again?

_____

_____

If dreaming about your parents reconciling creates positive feelings within you, what else can you do to create those same positive feelings?

_____

_____

_____

blaming one parent 15

for you to know

When parents divorce, teens often find themselves wanting to blame one parent or the other for the split. It can feel easier to label one parent the "bad guy" and one parent the "good guy." But in reality, neither parent is all bad or all good.

Nick spent hours thinking about his parents' divorce, repeatedly changing his mind about who was to blame. Most days he blamed his father. His father was never home and although he had a good income, he never gave Nick's mom any attention. Nick didn't blame his mom for getting fed up. But, some days Nick blamed his mom. She could be a really hard person to get along with. She was often short-tempered and was very picky about things. Nick wondered whether that was why his dad worked so much.

Laina blamed her mother completely for her parents' divorce. She and her mom had a hard time getting along, but Laina got along beautifully with her dad. When Laina was with her dad on the weekends, they did lots of fun activities like going to the mall or to a movie or out to eat. When she was with her mom, all her mom did was nag Laina about her homework, her chores, or her attitude. Laina's dad would buy her just about anything she wanted, and her mom never had any money to spare for her.

Nick and Laina were both angry that their parents got divorced. It can feel uncomfortable to hold that anger inside. One way to release it is to blame someone for the situation. Then all of the anger can be directed toward that one person.

It can also feel uncomfortable to feel anger toward both of your parents at the same time that your family is breaking up. Being angry at both parents may feel scarier than being angry at just one. Blaming one person for the divorce instead of both allowed Nick and Laina to stay emotionally attached to at least one part of their parental unit.

Thinking that one person has both positive and negative traits or behaviors can also feel uncomfortable or confusing. Sometimes it is easier to think of a person as all negative or all positive. Blaming one parent for the divorce can be an easier feeling to tolerate than seeing them each as having a part in it.

for you to do

In the first box below, write your mother's name, and then list all of her positive traits that you can think of. Next to that, list all her negative traits that you can think of. In the second box, write your father's name and list his positive and negative traits in the same way.

Positive Traits	Negative Traits		Positive Traits	Negative Traits

Circle any of your parents' traits that you think might have contributed to their divorce.

Explain any other factors about your mother and father that you think might have contributed to their divorce.

Mother	Father

...and more to do!

Do you blame one of your parents more than the other for their divorce? Explain why or why not.

_____

_____

_____

Describe how it feels to look at the situation in this way.

_____

_____

_____

Describe how it feels to think that each of your parents had something to do with the divorce, not just one.

_____

_____

_____

Think about the last time that you got into a disagreement with someone. How did each of you contribute to that disagreement?

_____

_____

_____

_____

Pretend you are your mother. Close your eyes and really try to think about what it feels like to be her. From her perspective, not yours, tell why you think she wanted to get divorced.

_____

_____

_____

_____

Pretend you are your father. Close your eyes and really try to think about what it feels like to be him. From his perspective, not yours, tell why you think he wanted to get divorced.

_____

_____

_____

_____

If it was hard to think from either of your parents' perspectives, or if you really couldn't imagine this, ask each of your parents to tell you their perspectives. Write their answers here.

_____

_____

_____

_____

_____

_____

16 blaming the divorce

for you to know

When parents get divorced, teens sometimes find themselves using the divorce as a scapegoat for all of their unhappiness; they blame the divorce for things they don't like about themselves or for other things that go wrong in their lives. This may feel good at first, but eventually it only makes things worse, not better.

Alex's life seemed to be getting worse and worse ever since his parents got divorced. At first his grades began to drop. Next he got caught smoking behind the school. Then he lied to his best friend and now his friend wasn't talking to him.

Alex's parents were concerned about him and asked him to see a counselor with them. During the counseling session, Alex got very upset and told his parents it was all their fault; if they hadn't gotten divorced, none of this would have happened.

The counselor told Alex it made sense that he was upset about the divorce, and that his sad or angry mood might affect how he was able to manage the rest of his life. She also said he had to learn how to cope with his feelings and take responsibility for his actions. It was he, not his parents, who had stopped studying, started smoking, and lied to his best friend.

Alex didn't like hearing what the counselor was saying. He told her it was too hard to make the right decisions or have the energy to keep his life on track when he felt so bad inside. It was easier to just give up and blame the divorce and his parents for ruining his life.

Alex and his parents continued working with the counselor for a number of weeks. During that time, the counselor helped Alex find healthy ways to express his feelings and to take care of himself when he felt bad. As a result, he had more energy to make better choices about his behavior. Alex was upset that his parents got divorced, but he realized that he couldn't blame the divorce for the choices he made. Using the divorce as a scapegoat had only made things worse.

for you to do

The teens in the pictures below are each blaming their parents' divorce for something they are unhappy about. Describe what is happening in each picture, and then explain what really caused this situation to occur.

_____

_____

_____

_____

_____

_____

_____

_____

_____

_____

_____

_____

_____

_____

_____

...and more to do!

Has anyone ever blamed you for something because they didn't want to take responsibility for their own actions? Describe what happened.

_____

_____

_____

Why do you think the person blamed you instead of taking responsibility?

_____

_____

_____

What does it feel like to take responsibility for things in your life that you aren't happy with?

_____

_____

_____

Why do you think taking responsibility can feel more difficult than blaming?

_____

_____

_____

_____

Make a list of anything you have blamed on your parents' divorce.

_____   _____

_____   _____

_____   _____

_____   _____

_____   _____

Circle the items on your list that are really the fault of the divorce.

Put an "R" next to the items on your list that are actually your responsibility.

Tell what you think will eventually happen if you continue to blame the divorce for the negative situations in your life.

_____

_____

_____

_____

_____

_____

_____

If you don't think you have the energy to take responsibility for your own actions, talk to a counselor or other adult about how you feel.

17 your feelings about marriage

for you to know

When parents divorce, teens may to start to question their feelings or beliefs about marriage and relationships. They might question ideas or plans they had for their own future. They might reconsider truths and values that they previously had thought were unshakable.

Jeana had been going steady with Brandon for three months. She was happy in their relationship and enjoyed the time they spent together. They liked a lot of the same activities, had most of the same friends, and wanted similar things in life. Jeana knew they were far too young to think about getting married, but she could see herself dating Brandon for a long time.

When her parents got divorced, Jeana found herself looking at Brandon differently. Their relationship scared her a little. She worried about tying herself down to one boy. She asked Brandon if he thought they should date other people instead of going steady. Jeana had always pictured herself getting married and having children of her own some day—after she'd graduated from college and had her own career. Now she wasn't sure. What if she got married and had children and it didn't work out? She never wanted to go through the pain that she saw her parents going through in their divorce. Everything seemed so impermanent all of a sudden. She found herself drawing away from Brandon, and even from her close girlfriends as well.

The next time she came to visit, Jeana's grandma asked how Brandon was. Jeana looked kind of sad. She shrugged and told her grandmother about all the doubts she suddenly had. Her grandmother told her it was normal to feel that way after seeing her parents' marriage end. But she also said that Jeana was a separate person from her parents and would make her own choices. Her grandmother reminded her of all the people she knew who had been married for a very long time and had not divorced. She and Jeana's grandfather had been married for forty years and had no plans to separate. She told Jeana that there were many benefits to committed relationships, but it was also wise to think carefully about the choices she would make.

for you to do

Five committed relationships are listed below. In the second column, rate your desire to have each relationship at some time in the future. Use a scale from 1 to 10, with 1 = not at all and 10 = more than anything. In the third column, rate your confidence in maintaining this relationship, with 1 = no confidence and 10 = complete confidence. In the fourth column, explain your choice.

Relationship	Having This Relationship	Maintaining This Relationship	Why I Chose This Rating
Dating			
Going Steady			
Living With a Committed Partner			
Engagement			
Marriage			

…and more to do!

Is your desire to have each of these relationships affected by your parents' divorce? Tell why, or why not.

_____

_____

_____

_____

Is your confidence in your ability to maintain each of these relationships affected by your parents' divorce? Tell why, or why not.

_____

_____

_____

_____

Tell whether any of your other ideas or values have been affected by your parents' divorce.

_____

_____

_____

_____

Describe how any of your current committed relationships have been affected by your parents' divorce.

_____

_____

_____

_____

Tell what skills you think are necessary to maintain a committed relationship.

_____

_____

_____

_____

_____

_____

_____

_____

_____

Write an "H" next to any of these skills that you think you already have.

Write a "D" next to any of these skills that you still need to develop.

18 your sexuality

for you to know

During adolescence, hormones are directing your body to grow and develop in new ways. These hormones cause changes in the way you look and feel. It is normal for sexual desire and sexual attraction to develop and increase at this time. These feelings and changes can be confusing, exciting, and scary. If your divorced parents start dating other people at this time, your feelings about your own sexuality can become even more challenging.

When Erica's parents had been divorced about a year, her dad started talking to her about a woman in his apartment building. He said he was attracted to this woman, and he shared a lot of his emotional and physical feelings with Erica, as if she were a friend, not a daughter. Erica was very uncomfortable with her dad telling her these things, but she didn't want to make him mad by telling him to stop.

When Deric's mom told him she was going on a date with a man she worked with, Deric was uncomfortable. He wondered what the date would involve, and didn't like thinking of his mom being affectionate with any man other than his father. He found himself becoming more aggressive with his girlfriend, both emotionally and physically. She became angry and told him to back off.

When Shiana's dad moved out of their house, Shiana found herself becoming more flirtatious with the boys in her class. She had never dated much, but now she started dressing differently and found many boys paying attention to her. It seemed that the more upset she was about not seeing her father, the more she flirted. Sometimes she felt uncomfortable with the way boys were beginning to look at her and with some of the things they said.

James's dad started dating a number of different women soon after he was divorced from James's mom. Frequently when James was visiting for the weekend, his dad would have a girlfriend spending the night. Sometimes James found himself having sexual thoughts about his dad's girlfriend. This made him feel confused, scared, and bad about himself. He wondered if there were something wrong with him.

Soon after Rachel's parents were divorced, she and her mother moved in with her mother's new boyfriend. Rachel was uncomfortable in this living situation. She started feeling uncomfortable with her own boyfriend as well. She hated that her body was developing and started restricting how much she ate in an attempt to keep her body thinner and more boyish looking.

The teens in these stories are all reacting to their parents dating. They are all trying to manage their uncomfortable feelings in one way or another. Some of them understand their feelings and some don't.

for you to do

Answer the questions about each teen. There are no right or wrong answers, only your opinion.

Why do you think Erica didn't like her dad talking about the woman he was attracted to?

_____

_____

_____

What could Erica do so her dad would stop talking about this?

Erica

_____

_____

_____

Why do you think Deric felt uncomfortable about his mom dating a man at work?

_____

_____

Deric

_____

Why do you think Deric started acting different toward his girlfriend?

_____

_____

_____

_____

Why do you think Shiana changed the way she acted around boys?

_____

_____

_____

Shiana

What could Shiana do when she didn't like the way boys were treating her?

_____

_____

_____

What do you think it was like for James to see his father with so many different women?

_____

_____

James

_____

Do you think there was something wrong with James? Explain your answer.

_____

_____

How do you think Rachel felt living with her mother and her mother's boyfriend?

_____

_____

Why do you think Rachel would want to stop her body from developing?

Rachel

_____

_____

...and more to do!

Answer the following questions using words from the list below. Add any of your own feelings that aren't shown here.

happy	apprehensive	annoyed	_____
guilty	stressed	embarrassed	_____
excited	scared	sad	_____
nervous	confused	angry	_____
jealous	surprised	anxious	_____
proud	worried	pleased	_____

How do you feel about the idea of your body developing during adolescence?

_____

_____

_____

How do you feel about the idea of your sexuality developing during adolescence?

_____

_____

_____

How do you feel about the thought of your mom dating?

_____

_____

_____

How do you feel about the thought of your dad dating?

_____

_____

_____

Explain how your mom or dad dating affects your feelings about your own sexuality.

_____

_____

_____

Explain how you have acted similar to or different from the teens in these stories.

Erica _____

_____

Deric _____

_____

Shiana _____

_____

James _____

_____

Rachel _____

_____

It is normal to feel many different feelings about your developing sexuality and also your parents' intimacy with other people. If these thoughts and feelings are bothering you, it can help to talk about them with a counselor or another adult whom you trust.

19 moving

for you to know

When parents divorce, there is almost always a change in living arrangements. Sometimes teens will be able to stay in their original home, but sometimes they will have to move to a new home. The idea of moving can feel upsetting, but it is possible to manage this change by using healthy coping skills.

Nigel was nervous. He and his mom and sister were going to be leaving the house he had grown up in and moving to another part of the city. It meant he would leave everything he was familiar with—his neighborhood, his school, and his friends. Nigel did not want to move, but no matter how much he argued with his mother, she would not change her mind. When she and Nigel's father divorced, they had agreed to sell the house. She couldn't afford another house in the same neighborhood, so they would have to move to an older part of the city, where the houses were less expensive.

Nigel's basketball coach noticed that Nigel had seemed distracted and on edge for a few weeks. After practice one night, he called Nigel into the gym office and asked if anything was wrong. Nigel told him what was happening and how he felt about it. Coach Brenner listened and said he understood. He knew what it was like to move because his father had been in the army and his own family had moved to a new house, and sometimes even to a new state, almost every year when he was a boy.

Nigel was amazed, and asked the coach how he had handled all those changes. Coach Brenner told Nigel that it was hard at first, but eventually he learned a strategy that helped him through. He said that if Nigel thought about the challenge of moving like the challenge of a basketball game, it could make things easier. Coach Brenner erased the team notes from his chalk board, and wrote this in their place:

Moving Strategy

1. Build your confidence. Think about past games that you've won or done well at. Make a list of all the previous challenges you have faced and met—from the furthest thing back, like learning to walk, to the most recent, like making the basketball team. Make the list as long as you can, and when you feel nervous about meeting the challenge of moving, remind yourself of all the other challenges you have successfully met before.

2. Focus on your team. Think of all the people who care about you and can help you meet this challenge. Call on them when you need to, just like you would your teammates in a game. Remember that you are not in this alone.

3. Stay in shape. Just like eating right, sleeping enough, and working out can help you be in your best shape for a basketball game, those behaviors can also help you to stay emotionally strong and balanced for the move. When you are physically healthy, it is easier to manage stress, think clearly, and stay calm.

4. Learn the details of your challenge. When you know something about the players on the opposing team in a game, you are more prepared to meet them. Learning something about the new place you will move to can prepare you for living there. Drive by your new house; visit your new school; talk to the coach of their basketball team and see if you want to try out. The more you know about your new location, the more familiar and less daunting it will be.

5. Be yourself. If you are great at passing but have a hard time dribbling the ball down the court, you will have more success when you stick to passing. When you go to a new school and meet new kids, be true to yourself instead of trying to be someone you're not. Develop and celebrate the natural strengths of your personality, and you will be a player that people like to have on their team.

for you to do

This page below shows the notes that Nigel made with Coach Brenner for his personal moving strategy. On the next page, fill in your own notes to prepare yourself for a move.

○ 1. Past challenges I have met: learning to walk, learning to talk, going to school for the first time, learning how to read and write, learning how to swim, learning how to ride a bike, learning how to play basketball, trying out for the basketball team, bringing up my English grade, passing algebra, asking Alysha to the dance, being a camp counselor, painting our garage

2. People I could call on for help: Mom, Dad, Coach Brenner, Uncle Mark, Mr. Simmons next door, grandparents, my best friend Jared, my former Cub Scout leader

○ 3. How I can stay in shape: get to bed before midnight, remember to eat breakfast, work out after school

4. How I can learn about my new neighborhood: look at the school's Web site and check their basketball record, team, and statistics; drive around the new neighborhood and look for nearest outdoor basketball courts

○ 5. Strengths of my personality: good friend, good joke-teller, honest, polite, team player, sometimes courageous

1. Past challenges I have met:

○

2. People I could call on for help:

3. How I can stay in shape:

○

4. How I can learn about the new neighborhood:

○ 5. Strengths of my personality:

○

...and more to do!

Circle any of the phrases below that describe what you think makes moving hard or uncomfortable.

having to make new friends   leaving familiar surroundings

having to start a new school   leaving neighbors

not knowing what the future will hold   wondering if new kids will like you

leaving a home you liked   moving all of your possessions

wondering if you will make good grades   missing your old friends

Explain anything else that is difficult for you about having to move.

_____

_____

_____

Which of the moving strategy coping skills that Coach Brenner gave Nigel do you think might help you?

_____

_____

_____

Describe the house you live in now. Tell how long you have lived there.

_____

_____

Make a list of some of your favorite memories that took place in this house.

_____

_____

_____

Explain what you will miss the most about this house, neighborhood, or town.

_____

_____

_____

Describe the home you will move to when your parents get divorced.

_____

_____

_____

Make a list of some of the good times that you hope will happen in the future in your new home.

_____

_____

_____

Pretend that it is one year in the future and you have been living in your new home for a long time now. Describe some of the positive things that you might be saying now that you are adjusted to this new place.

_____

_____

20 living in two homes

for you to know

The most common living change that occurs as the result of a divorce is that parents who once lived together now live in separate homes. Depending on how custody is arranged, teens might end up living part-time with each parent. This can feel disruptive and confusing at first, but with time a new routine sets in and the change begins to feel more normal.

Cassie felt like she was going crazy. One weekend she was at her dad's house, and the next weekend she was at her mom's. Every Wednesday after soccer practice she had dinner and spent the night at her dad's, and he drove her to the school bus stop in her mom's neighborhood the next morning. Sometimes Cassie would forget whose house she was sleeping at when. Sometimes she would leave her homework at her dad's and couldn't get it for another week unless she made a special trip to pick it up. Sometimes her purple sweater was in her dresser at her dad's when she wanted it, and sometimes she remembered it was in the laundry at her mom's.

One Saturday when Cassie was at her violin lesson, she realized she had left the music she needed at her mom's house. She was upset and angry. Lynda, her violin teacher, asked what was going on. Cassie told her that ever since her parents got divorced she felt disrupted on the inside and disrupted on the outside. Nothing was the way it was supposed to be or where it was supposed to be, including her parents. She hated living in two houses; it was confusing and made her feel very emotional. She wished her family hadn't split up. She wished that everything was peaceful again and that she had only one bed to sleep in instead of two.

Lynda told Cassie that it made sense she was feeling that way. There had been a major change in her life, and she wasn't used to it yet. It was confusing to live in two houses. The two houses were also a reminder of an emotional wound—the fact that her parents were divorced.

She asked if Cassie remembered when she had first started violin lessons, four years ago. Everything had seemed confusing to her then, too. She had to remember which strings were which notes, and which way to place her fingers at which times. She often forgot how to hold her bow and sometimes even forgot to bring it to her lesson. The first time she had to memorize a piece, she thought she would never get it right. Lynda reminded Cassie that what had helped her manage everything was getting organized and practicing. Cassie had started writing down what she had to remember. She started keeping her bow and violin and her music together in one place all the time so she wouldn't forget one. She began to practice her lessons on a regular basis.

Lynda sat down with Cassie, and they made a list of all the things she needed to keep at her dad's house—like a toothbrush, her favorite shampoo, and extra notebook paper for homework. Cassie would ask her dad to buy these things and always keep them in supply at his house. Then they made a list of everything that Cassie needed to remember to bring when she visited him. That included things like current homework assignments and clothes for the weekend. Then Lynda helped Cassie go through her assignment notebook and write in every day for the next few months that Cassie would visit her dad. That way, when she looked to see what homework she had due, she would also see whose house she was to stay at.

Cassie said that being organized helped, but it didn't change the upset she felt from her parents living separately. Lynda said that was the harder part of divorce, so it would take longer to get used to, but even that would get better with practice and time.

for you to do

The list below describes different aspects of living in two houses that many teens don't like. Rate each item from 1–5 to tell how much it bothers you in your own life. (1 = very little and 5 = very much)

					How Long It May Take to Get Used to This
Having to leave friends on certain days	1 2 3 4			5	_____
Watching parents argue when they drop you off	1 2 3 4			5	_____
Having to remember different rules at each house	1 2 3 4			5	_____
Being with only one parent at a time	1 2 3 4			5	_____
Having to pack your things all the time	1 2 3 4			5	_____
Feeling like you can never just relax and stay in one place	1 2 3 4			5	_____
Having to remember what to bring from house to house	1 2 3 4			5	_____
Having to remember two phone numbers and addresses	1 2 3 4			5	_____
Being comfortable in one house but not the other	1 2 3 4			5	_____
Having your social life interrupted	1 2 3 4			5	_____
Not having friends at one house	1 2 3 4			5	_____

Add to this list anything else that is difficult for you about having to live in two houses.

_____

_____

_____

Choose three of the items from your list that you gave the highest score. Write about each in more detail, explaining how you feel about it and why it affects you so much.

_____

_____

_____

_____

_____

_____

_____

_____

_____

Next to each item that you rated, write a guess as to how long you think it will take you to get used to this and not have it bother you as much.

...and more to do!

Cassie solved part of her problem by becoming more organized. Tell what you could do to be more organized and make living in two homes a little easier.

_____

_____

_____

Circle any of the situations below that you have experienced and didn't like at first, but eventually got used to.

the birth of a sibling   getting a job   doing homework

going to school   someone you love dying   a particular class

doing chores   sharing a room   losing a friend

List any other situations in your life that you didn't like at first but eventually got used to.

_____

_____

_____

Next to each item, write approximately how long it took you to get used to it.

Do you think you will ever get used to your parents living separately? Explain your answer.

_____

_____

_____

When T.J.'s parents got divorced, his father moved out of state, so far that T.J. was only able to visit him on long school holidays and during summer vacation.

Claire's parents lived in the same town, and even though they were divorced, they got along well. Claire's mother let her visit her father whenever she wanted to.

Evan had chosen to live with his father when his parents divorced. He stayed with his mother every other weekend and on Wednesday nights.

Holly's parents lived about an hour away from each other. Holly was supposed to visit her dad every weekend, but very often her mother was angry at her father and wouldn't let her go to see him.

Paul's parents had joint custody of him. Paul lived with his mother for one half of the week and with his father for the other half.

There are many different ways to work out visitation schedules. Sometimes teens can help decide what the visitation will be, sometimes not. Sometimes parents adhere strictly to the schedule, sometimes they ignore it completely. Most of the time, teens must do what their parents decide.

for you to do

In this yearly calendar, create your ideal visitation schedule. Using one color pencil or ink, write an "M" on all the days you would like to live with your mother and an "F" on all the days you would like to live with your father. It doesn't have to actually be possible: Just think about what you would do if you could have visitation the exact way you wanted it to be.

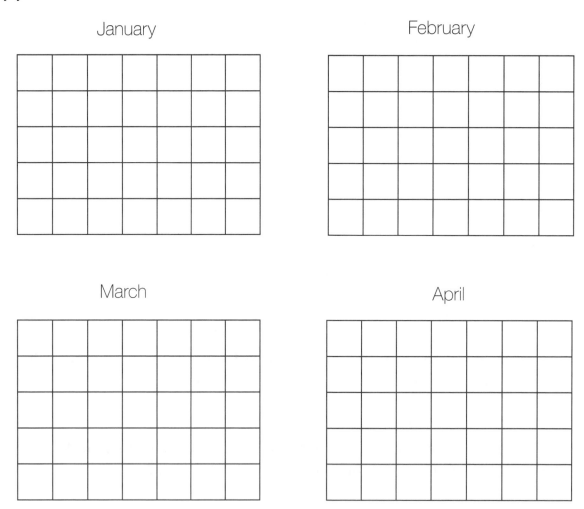

January   February

March   April

May

June

July

August

September

October

November

December

Then, using a second color pencil or ink, go back and write in the way your actual visitation schedule looks.

Describe the differences between your ideal calendar and your real calendar.

_____

_____

_____

Explain why you think you do or do not have to accept these differences.

_____

_____

_____

Explain what it is like for you to have to accept the differences that you do.

_____

_____

_____

...and more to do!

Look back over the examples of the other teens' visitation schedules. Tell what you would like or not like about each of their schedules.

T.J. _____

_____

Claire _____

_____

Evan _____

_____

Holly _____

_____

Paul _____

_____

Explain what is the hardest part about visitation for you.

_____

_____

_____

_____

_____

Sometimes teens eventually find positive aspects of visitation. For example:

- T.J. liked that he could stay with his dad for a long stretch of time because they could take camping trips together.

- Claire liked the fact that her parents got along better now that they didn't have to live in the same house.

- Evan liked living with his dad because even though he loved his mom, his dad was easier to get along with as a roommate.

- Holly liked that when she did see her dad, she was far away from her mom and could forget about the problems she sometimes had with her.

- Paul liked that he had made friends near both of his parents' homes, so he ended having twice as many friends as if he only lived in one place.

Describe anything that you think is or could be positive about your visitation arrangement.

_____

_____

_____

_____

_____

for you to know

When parents divorce, it is common for their financial situation to change. When they live apart, they have to pay for two separate households. Sometimes teens worry about whether their parents will have enough money to continue caring for them the way they used to.

When Miguel's parents told him they were getting divorced, they explained that his father would move into a condo, and he and his mother and sister would continue to live in their house. To afford this, however, his mother would have to go back to work, and they would also have to cut back on some expenses.

Learning about this financial change worried Miguel a great deal. He wondered if his mom could make enough money to pay all the expenses on the house, and if she couldn't, he wondered what would happen. He wondered if he would still be able to take drum lessons and if he and his sister would still be able to have their own cell phones. He remembered his parents complaining about the cable television bill and the cost of high-speed Internet service. He wondered what was going to change in his life because of their change in finances. He wondered if he would have to start giving his mom his lawn-mowing money to help out.

His mom noticed that Miguel often seemed nervous. She asked him what was wrong and he told her the things he was worried about. His mom sat down and talked to him in more detail about the situation. With a calculator, she went over both the income and the bills and showed him that her new job would allow them to stay in the house. But she also showed him that there wouldn't be as much extra money. She said that she and Miguel and his sister would decide together what cutbacks they would make. They could all think about what was most important to them, and what they could most easily give up.

Miguel's mom also reminded him that even if they had to give up some material things, the important things in his life were still in place: His parents loved him very much; he was healthy and strong; he was a talented drummer and a good student; he had friends who cared about him and liked to be with him. These were things that money couldn't buy.

When Miguel knew more specifically about the finances, he felt a little better. He was relieved to know they could afford to live in the house and glad that he would have some choice in the things he would have to give up. He realized that if he mowed two extra lawns each week, he could afford to pay his own cell phone bill. He also knew that his mom was right about material things. They were nice, but there were other things even more important that didn't depend upon a certain income.

for you to do

Next to each dollar sign, write the name of something you might have to give up if your parents' divorce decreases the amount of money they have to spend on you. Go back and number these items from 1–5, with 1 being the hardest to give up and 5 being the easiest. Next to each item, explain your reasoning.

$ _____   _____

$ _____   _____

$ _____   _____

$ _____   _____

$ _____   _____

Next to each heart shape, write the name of something that you will not have to give up because it can't be purchased with money. Go back and number these items from 1–5, with 1 being the hardest to give up and 5 being the easiest. Next to each item, explain your reasoning.

♥ _____   _____

♥ _____   _____

♥ _____   _____

♥ _____   _____

♥ _____   _____

...and more to do!

Explain why you would or would not be comfortable talking to your parents about finances the way Miguel did.

_____

_____

_____

Tell what you worry might happen if your parents' financial situation changes because of their divorce.

_____

_____

Is it fair that you might have to give up some material things because your parents got divorced? Explain your answer.

_____

_____

Describe how you would handle it if you had to give up the top two items on your dollar list.

_____

_____

Describe what it would be like if you had to give up the top two items on your heart list.

_____

_____

_____

for you to know

All feelings come from thoughts. Because no one else can tell you what to think, you control your own thoughts, which means that you also control your own feelings. Choosing to have positive thoughts and a positive attitude can help you cope with your parents' divorce.

Justin and Jennifer were twins whose parents were getting divorced. While they looked very much alike, they thought very differently. Because of this, they experienced their parents' divorce very differently.

Justin was very upset about the divorce. He was angry at his mom and dad, and he felt sad. He told himself that his parents had ruined his life. He told himself that because his home had been broken, he would have more problems in the future. He told himself that he would be very unhappy having to visit his mom only on the weekends. He told himself that his social life would be disrupted and he might not be able to be on the baseball team this year. Justin started having a hard time getting out of bed in the morning and paying attention in class. He didn't go out with his friends as often. His grades started dropping, and his friends stopped calling.

Jennifer was also very upset about her parents' divorce. She was angry at her mom and dad, and she felt sad, just like Justin. However, Jennifer told herself different things than Justin did. Jennifer told herself that there was a big change in her life, but she still had a lot of things to be happy about. She told herself that she could learn from her parents' mistakes and make different choices about marriage in her own life. She told herself that if her parents lived separately, she wouldn't have to hear them argue all the time. Jennifer talked about her sadness with her friends, but she continued to go out with them. When she found it hard to concentrate on homework, she would write about her feelings in a journal, and then had more energy to work again.

Both Justin and Jennifer were going through a hard time, but they were having different experiences of it because of their attitudes and the thoughts that they chose.

for you to do

These teens are all facing situations that they initially don't like. Their experience of the situation will depend on how they choose to think about it. Below each picture, write a thought that would make the teen feel better, and a thought that would make the teen feel worse.

Positive thought

_____

_____

_____

_____

Negative thought

_____

_____

_____

Positive thought

_____

_____

_____

Negative thought

_____

_____

_____

Positive thought

_____

_____

_____

_____

Negative thought

_____

_____

_____

_____

Positive thought

_____

_____

_____

_____

Negative thought

_____

_____

_____

_____

...and more to do!

List three upsetting things that happened in the past year. Then write some thoughts you could have chosen that would have made you feel positive rather than negative about each situation.

1. _____   _____

    _____

2. _____   _____

    _____

3. _____   _____

    _____

List three things that happened in the past year that you were very happy about. Then write some thoughts you could have chosen that would have made you feel negative rather than positive about the situation.

1. _____   _____

    _____

2. _____   _____

    _____

3. _____   _____

    _____

Your attitude is a very powerful tool, which only you can control. List three negative thoughts you could have about your parents' divorce that would make you feel upset.

1. _____

2. _____

3. _____

Now choose to have a positive attitude instead, and list three positive thoughts that you could have about your parents' divorce.

1. _____

2. _____

3. _____

Choosing positive thoughts does not mean ignoring upsetting feelings. But choosing positive thoughts can help you to move past your upsetting feelings. List any upsetting feelings that you have about your parents' divorce.

_____

_____

_____

Explain how changing your thoughts could help you to move past each of these feelings.

_____

_____

_____

24 things that don't change

"My whole life is changing!" Yolanda complained to her counselor. "I don't know what I'm going to do. Everything is different, and I don't know who I am anymore. My family is broken up and my heart hurts and I'm mad. I feel like there's been an earthquake in my life."

Yolanda's counselor said she understood how Yolanda must be feeling. When parents get divorced, it can seem like the whole world is splitting apart, not just the family. Thinking of that would be frightening and unsettling for anyone. Then the counselor asked Yolanda if there were anything at all that would not change in her life when her parents divorced.

At first Yolanda said no, but then she thought some more and said, "Well, I get to keep my dog." "How do you feel when you think about keeping your dog?" the counselor asked. Yolanda smiled for the first time. "That feels much more peaceful," she said.

The counselor pointed out that when Yolanda focused her thoughts on the things that were going to change, she felt unsettled. But when she focused on something that wasn't going to change, she felt peaceful. She asked Yolanda to go home and write down as many things as she could think of that were not going to change when her parents divorced. Yolanda thought that it wouldn't take very long, but once she started writing, she realized that there were many things that would not change.

She showed her list to the counselor the next day. They talked about trying to focus on the things that would not change as a way to help Yolanda feel more peaceful. Each time she started feeling unsettled about something that would change, she shifted her focus to something that would not change. Yolanda realized that she had learned a way to help herself feel more stable.

Yolanda's list of things that wouldn't change included the following items:

○ 1. my name

2. my birthday

3. my best friend

4. my dog

5. my piano lessons

6. my soccer team

7. my favorite teacher

○ 8. my favorite color

9. pizza night with Grandma

10. going to the pool in summer

11. my sister

12. my parents' love for me

○ 13. my curly hair

14. my green eyes

15. my cousins

16. the guy I like in English class

for you to do

In the picture of the peaceful clouds below, write the things that will not change about your life when your parents get divorced.

...and more to do!

Look at the picture of the clouds and everything you have identified that will not change. On the scale below, rate your level of peacefulness when you think about these things that will remain the same.

unsettled						peaceful			
1	2	3	4	5	6	7	8	9	10

Think about something that will change or has changed because of your parents' divorce, and on the next scale, rate your level of peacefulness when you think about this.

unsettled						peaceful			
1	2	3	4	5	6	7	8	9	10

Compare your two scales and describe what you see as you look at them.

_____

_____

_____

_____

_____

How do you think you will feel if you continue to focus on the things that will change?

_____

_____

_____

_____

How do you think you will feel if you continue to focus on the things that will not change?

_____

_____

_____

_____

Tell why you think it might be hard to focus only on the things that will not change.

_____

_____

_____

_____

_____

Explain why everyone has a choice about which thoughts they choose to think.

_____

_____

_____

_____

25 physical exercise

for you to know

Physical exercise helps release the tension that builds up in our bodies when we experience stress. Participating in some form of physical exercise can help you to better cope with the stressful feelings you experience in reaction to your parents' divorce.

When the human body experiences stress, the brain sends a signal to the glands to release certain hormones that prepare us to either run from the stressor or fight it. These hormones cause our muscles to tense, our pupils to dilate, and our hearts to beat faster. Physically, we are ready to protect ourselves from danger.

The stress of experiencing a parents' divorce causes these hormones to release, and if we don't expel that fight-or-flight energy, it stays in our bodies, causing chronic aches and pains or tension. One of the best ways to dissipate stress is through physical exertion. Exercise not only burns off the stress hormones, but it also causes the release of endorphins, which are hormones that make us feel relaxed and happy.

When you participate in some kind of physical exercise, whether it is a team sport, something you do by yourself, or with one or two friends, you are using your body to help you cope with stress, both emotionally and physically. Participating in a physical activity that you enjoy can take your mind off what is stressing you, reduce the stress hormones in your body, and help your brain send out endorphins that make you feel good again.

for you to do

The list below describes a number of physical activities that create exercise for the body. Put a star next to any of the activities that you currently enjoy. Circle any of the activities that you would like to try. Draw a line through any of the activities that you do not enjoy or would not want to try.

baseball	basketball	skiing	swimming
hiking	tennis	biking	snowboarding
football	karate	running	bowling
gymnastics	wrestling	archery	golf
paintball	badminton	judo	water-skiing
volleyball	laser tag	dance	racewalking
tubing	lacrosse	soccer	bocce ball
diving	surfing	kickboxing	lifting weights
racquetball	rappelling	aerobic dance	windsurfing

Write down any other physical activities that you enjoy.

_____

_____

_____

_____

_____

_____

...and more to do!

Exercise can be practiced both as prevention and intervention. Prevention means that you exercise on a regular basis, whether you feel particularly stressed or not. Preventative exercise keeps your baseline stress level lower. Then, when something stressful happens, your stress level will not go as high. List any activities that you could do for prevention.

_____

_____

_____

_____

Tell when and where you could realistically do these activities.

_____

_____

_____

_____

When you exercise at a time that you feel highly stressed, you are using exercise for intervention. List any activities that you could do for intervention at times when you notice your stress level going very high.

_____

_____

_____

_____

Describe any times in the past when you have felt yourself become very stressed about your parents' divorce.

_____

_____

_____

_____

_____

_____

Which of the above activities could you have done at these times to help lower your stress level?

_____

_____

_____

People often have good intentions about exercising, but they set their goals too high and then have trouble meeting them. Be sure to set exercise goals that are very realistic so they can actually help you.

26 peaceful movement

for you to know

Peaceful movement, such as relaxed stretching, yoga, or tai chi, can help release tension and stress from your body. Practicing any of these activities can help you cope with and release upsetting feelings about your parents' divorce.

Relaxed stretching is the gentle, sustained movement of lengthening your muscles. When you stretch your muscles, you help dissipate stress chemicals that have built up in your body. You also increase your blood flow and improve your circulation. These changes can help you feel more peaceful, both physically and emotionally. Practicing relaxed stretching when you first wake up in the morning can bring blood to your muscle groups and help you feel energized. Stretching right before you go to bed can release tension and help you sleep better. Stretching at a time of high stress or emotion can help release your uncomfortable feelings in a healthy way.

Yoga is a series of movements and postures that attempt to unify body, mind, and spirit and help practitioners maintain balance and health in life. Yoga helps release stress by combining focused, peaceful movement with focused concentration and breathwork. The goal of yoga is to develop inner peace. Most people need some initial formal instruction through classes or videos to get started in yoga, but the basic movements and postures are designed for all levels, and the philosophy of yoga stresses noncompetitiveness. Practicing yoga can help you manage both the physical and emotional stresses you may experience when your parents divorce.

Tai chi is a practice of peaceful movement that seeks to stimulate the flow of chi, or energy throughout the body. The benefits of tai chi include creating a calm and tranquil mind, helping you relax and relieve tension, and reversing the effects of stress on your body and mind. Movements of tai chi are performed softly and gracefully with smooth, even transitions between them. Like yoga, tai chi initially requires some instruction from a class or video, but once you learn them, you can practice the movements on your own. You can use tai chi movements to help you relieve any physical or emotional stress that you experience as a result of your parents' divorce.

for you to do

Practices of peaceful movement can help you, but they only work if you learn them and then put some time into practice. Over the next few weeks, see if you can try each of these practices at least once. You can get help with basic instruction by taking a formal class, renting or buying a video or DVD, asking your physical education teacher for direction, or getting personal direction from someone you know who already practices these movements.

After you try each practice, describe your experience here.

Where I got instruction on relaxed stretching: _____

What kinds of stretches I tried: _____

How this movement made me feel physically: _____

How this movement made me feel emotionally: _____

Where I got instruction on yoga: _____

What types of yoga postures and movements I tried: _____

How this movement made me feel physically: _____

How this movement made me feel emotionally: _____

Where I got instruction in tai chi: _____

What types of tai chi movements I tried: _____

How this movement made me feel physically: _____

How this movement made me feel emotionally: _____

Which movement I would be willing to try again: _____

Which movement I would be willing to practice on a regular basis: _____

Which movement I really did not like: _____

The next time I will practice peaceful movement: _____

...and more to do!

Many people are not used to moving slowly. Explain why you think that is so.

_____

_____

Peaceful movement can help you relieve stress at the time you are feeling it. Describe a situation in the past week where you could have used some type of peaceful movement to calm yourself or relieve stress.

_____

_____

When peaceful movement is practiced over time, the benefits increase by helping you remain calm through all the moments of your life. Explain how you could realistically incorporate peaceful movement practice into your daily life—just like brushing your teeth or taking a shower.

_____

_____

Describe one stressful emotion or situation you've experienced in reaction to your parents' divorce that you think might be helped by peaceful movement.

_____

_____

Tell why you think that slow, peaceful movement is or is not helpful for you in reducing stress.

_____

_____

27 breathwork

for you to know

When you feel stressed, your breath is usually shallow and fast. When you feel calm, your breath is deeper and more steady. You can use your breath to help you relax and handle upsetting thoughts and feelings about your parents' divorce.

Juan's parents had been divorced for two weeks, and Juan found himself feeling nervous and distracted both at school and with his friends. He always seemed to feel anxious, even when there wasn't anything for him to be anxious about.

Juan didn't know what was wrong with him, so he asked his uncle Marcus, who was a doctor, what he could do to do to stop the nervousness. Uncle Marcus asked Juan if there was anything that had been upsetting him lately. Juan told him there was nothing—except his parents getting divorced, but that was already over. Marcus asked if there was any time when Juan did not feel anxious. Juan said yes: when he was running track or when he first woke up in the morning. Uncle Marcus said it was likely that Juan's anxiety was due to his still being upset about the divorce. He also said that Juan might not feel it when he was running or waking up because at those times his breathing was deeper and more steady than average. Marcus explained that deep, steady breathing brings oxygen into our bodies and relieves feelings of anxiety. He suggested that Juan practice some breathing exercises. He had his nurse e-mail Juan the exercises, and suggested he try them each a few times to see which would work best for him.

Juan followed his uncle's advice, and he found that when he did a few minutes of breathwork before school in the morning, he felt better throughout the day. If he felt himself getting anxious or distracted during the day, he did a simple breathing exercise right on the spot, and it helped him relax and focus again. He liked the exercises because he could do them at any time or in any situation and no one even noticed what he was doing.

for you to do

Here are the breathing exercises that Uncle Marcus's nurse sent Juan. Try each one yourself at least one time. Then record your reactions to the exercise.

Follow Your Breath

Sit quietly and comfortably and close your eyes. Try to locate your breath in your body, wherever it is. You may feel it moving into your nostrils, you may feel it in your throat or chest, or you may feel it all the way down in your abdomen or diaphragm. If you cannot seem to locate your breath, try holding it for a second or two. When you start breathing again you will be very aware of where it is. Once you find your breath, simply put your attention on it, and follow it wherever it goes as it moves in and out of your body. You don't have to try to change its pattern; simply follow it. Continue to follow your breath as it moves through your body for a couple of minutes. As you become more comfortable doing this exercise, you will find that as you focus on your breath, it will naturally become more steady and deep.

What this exercise felt like for me physically: _____

What this exercise felt like for me emotionally: _____

What I liked about this exercise: _____

What I did not like about this exercise: _____

activity 27 ✳ breathwork

Deeper Breathing

Sit quietly and comfortably and close your eyes. Take as deep a breath as you can through your nose. Hold it for a second or two. Then let the breath out as slowly as you can through your mouth. Repeat these steps two or three times. You can stop here, or continue repeating the steps until you feel all anxiety or stress gone from your body and mind.

What this exercise felt like for me physically: _____

What this exercise felt like for me emotionally: _____

What I liked about this exercise: _____

What I did not like about this exercise: _____

Releasing Negatives

Sit quietly and comfortably and close your eyes. As you take a deep breath in, picture yourself drawing peace into your body and mind. You might picture positive thoughts or pictures flowing in with your breath. Hold your breath for a second, and then exhale slowly. As you let your breath out, picture yourself breathing all negative or stressful thoughts and feelings out of your body and mind. You might picture any upsetting thoughts or feelings about your parents' divorce being exhaled with your breath and disappearing off into thin air. Repeat the positive inhale and the negative exhale as many times as you feel comfortable.

What this exercise felt like for me physically: _____

What this exercise felt like for me emotionally: _____

What I liked about this exercise: _____

What I did not like about this exercise: _____

...and more to do!

Sitting quietly and paying attention to our breath is something that many people are not used to doing. It can feel unfamiliar and uncomfortable at first. Rate how comfortable or uncomfortable it felt for you to do each exercise.

Follow Your Breath

1	2	3	4	5
uncomfortable				comfortable

Deeper Breathing

1	2	3	4	5
uncomfortable				comfortable

Releasing Negatives

1	2	3	4	5
uncomfortable				comfortable

Some teens discover that breathwork takes their mind off upsetting thoughts and feelings about their parents' divorce. Other teens say that it makes them think about the divorce more. Describe what happened to your upsetting thoughts when you tried these exercises.

_____

_____

_____

_____

Some teens say that breathwork helps them feel relaxed, but they don't think they would actually practice the exercises for the following reasons:

_____ I would be embarrassed to do these exercises.

_____ I don't have time to do these exercises.

_____ These exercises are not fun.

_____ These exercises are too different from the things I normally do.

_____ These exercises feel like a chore.

_____ I would not remember to do these exercises.

Put your initials next to any of these reasons that apply to you. Explain any other reasons why you might not do these exercises even if they are helpful.

_____

_____

_____

There are many things you might do on a daily basis even though they are not always entertaining or convenient: brushing your teeth, showering, household chores, homework, and taking a class that you have no interest in. Explain why you think people do things even though they are not entertaining or convenient.

_____

_____

_____

Explain why you might practice breathwork even if it is not entertaining or convenient.

_____

_____

_____

for you to know

When teens feel angry or upset about their parents getting divorced, they often want to avoid both their feelings and their parents. However, communicating with your parents in a healthy way can actually help you relieve and release difficult feelings.

Lakeisha was so upset about her parents' divorce that she sometimes felt like she would burst. But when her parents tried to talk to her about it, she changed the subject. She felt like they had already hurt her so much by getting divorced that she didn't trust them not to hurt her again. She avoided talking to them as much as possible so the subject couldn't come up. This behavior made her parents worry.

Lakeisha's mother had been seeing a counselor every other week to help her handle her own struggles with the divorce. When she told the counselor her concerns about her daughter, the counselor said that the other family members might also be holding in thoughts or feelings. They decided to make a counseling appointment for the whole family. Lakeisha's father and younger brother agreed to go along. The counselor told the family that it was normal to have communication problems during a divorce. It was a challenging time, and most people had strong feelings about what was happening. It could feel uncomfortable or even overwhelming to talk about those emotions. However, talking about them could also help release them, and even help heal relationships between family members.

As Lakeisha's family talked with the counselor, they began to share their feelings about the divorce. It felt safer to say these things in the counselor's office than at home. Lakeisha shared how angry she was; her brother told how scared he was. Her parents shared their sadness at the ending of their marriage. Hearing each other's feelings helped Lakeisha's family feel more caring towards each other and understand each other more.

They continued to see the counselor several more times. The more Lakeisha talked with her parents, the less angry she felt, and the better she got along with her teachers and friends. She still didn't like the fact that her parents were getting divorced, but her feelings were more manageable. Eventually, the family stopped seeing the counselor, but they agreed to continue talking to each other more at home.

for you to do

The teens in these pictures are experiencing different feelings about their parents' divorce. They are not talking to their parents about these feelings, and this is causing problems. Next to each picture, tell what you think the teen is feeling, what problem is being caused by not sharing their feelings, and how the situation might get better if they did talk with their parents

Teen's feeling: _____

Problem caused: _____

What could get better if feelings were shared: _____

Teen's feeling: _____

Problem caused: _____

What could get better if feelings were shared: _____

Teen's feeling: _____

Problem caused: _____

What could get better if feelings were shared: _____

_____

Teen's feeling: _____

Problem caused: _____

What could get better if feelings were shared: _____

_____

...and more to do!

Explain why you think it can be hard to talk about your feelings with your parents.

_____

_____

_____

_____

Describe any thoughts or feelings you have that you are apprehensive about sharing with your parents.

_____

_____

_____

_____

What do you think might happen if you shared these thoughts and feelings with your parents?

_____

_____

_____

Why do you think Lakeisha would talk to her parents in the counselor's office, but not at home?

_____

_____

_____

Describe any problems that are occurring because you are not communicating with your parents.

_____

_____

_____

_____

Tell what you would say to your parents if you felt safe enough to do so.

_____

_____

_____

_____

Talk with your counselor or another adult about the possibility of sharing these thoughts or feelings with your parents. Think about what circumstances would make you feel more comfortable doing this (for example, with one parent at a time, in a counselor's office, while you are driving in the car, or while you are watching TV together). Make a plan to communicate with your parents when you would feel most comfortable doing so. Tell what happens here.

_____

_____

_____

_____

for you to know

When you are going through your parents' divorce, one of your greatest resources for support is within you. Whether you realize it or not, you have many strengths and coping skills already in place, and you have used them already in other life situations. Identifying and mobilizing these strengths can help you support yourself.

It is normal to feel shaken or upset when your parents get divorced. You may feel like you will not be able to get over this change, or that you cannot handle the feelings you are experiencing. It is important to remember the strengths and coping skills that you carry within you that can help you through this time.

Teens are not always aware of, or used to paying attention to, their inner strengths. Once you identify the abilities that you possess to handle difficult situations, you can build your confidence and also use these abilities to your advantage.

Very often, you will discover that you have a greater capacity than you realized for handling life's challenges. Every time you identify and use your healthy coping skills, you strengthen them and build confidence in your ability to get through difficult situations. You will realize that you are not defenseless against the challenges you face.

for you to do

Each of the phrases below describes a coping skill that teens might use to help them through a difficult time. Circle any of those that you believe you already possess.

taking deep breaths to calm down   taking a break when I need it

seeing the bigger picture   expressing my feelings appropriately

asking for help when I need it   not giving up

accepting imperfection   being gentle with myself

planning ahead   taking one step at a time

seeing that I have choices   trying to see the other's point of view

thinking clearly   staying calm when necessary

focusing on the positive   breaking problems down into small parts

Add any other strengths you have that are not listed here.

_____

_____

_____

_____

_____

_____

...and more to do!

Describe a time in the past when you faced a challenge and used your strengths or coping skills to help you through.

_____

_____

_____

_____

List three other challenges you have survived in your life. After each one, write one coping skill that helped you through.

_____

_____

_____

Tell which part of your parents' divorce is the hardest for you to handle.

_____

_____

_____

_____

_____

Explain which of your current coping skills or inner strengths could help you handle this, and how.

_____

_____

_____

_____

Everyone can always learn more about how to take care of themselves. Which coping skills and strengths do you still need to acquire?

_____

_____

_____

_____

How could you learn these additional skills?

_____

_____

_____

_____

Counselors are people who are professionally trained to help others with personal challenges. If your parents' divorce is bothering you and you would like some help finding ways to feel better, a counselor can help you do that. Conversations between counselors and their clients are confidential.

Hannah's parents had been divorced for a year already, but every weekend when she went to her dad's house, Hannah was again reminded of how hurt she felt that her parents were no longer together. It was often in the back of her mind, and sometimes she found herself crying just before she went to sleep at night. She felt like such a baby and told herself to just get over it, but pushing the feelings down didn't seem to make them go away.

One day at swim practice, Hannah's coach approached her for a private conversation in the gym office. Coach Kelly said that Hannah wasn't swimming as well as she used to and she wondered if something was bothering her. Hannah told her about the feelings of sadness she still had about her parents' divorce, and Coach Kelly asked if she had ever talked to a counselor. Hannah said she would never do that; the other kids would make fun of her. Coach Kelly told Hannah that many healthy, high-functioning people talk to counselors. She told Hannah that she herself used to suffer from anxiety and panic attacks, and a counselor had helped her learn how to manage them. Now she rarely had them anymore.

Hannah was amazed. Coach Kelly was one of the smartest, nicest people she knew. Hannah would never have thought of her as having any problems like that. Coach Kelly said that no matter what it looks like from the outside, every single person has some challenge to deal with. Seeing a counselor for help is not a sign of weakness, but a sign of strength. It takes courage to face one's problems instead of hiding from them. Coach Kelly gave Hannah the name of a counselor who had experience working with teens, and Hannah's mother made an appointment for her the next week.

Once Hannah started talking with the counselor, she realized that Coach Kelly had been right. Hannah was gaining confidence in herself by expressing her feelings and finding healthy ways to deal with them. She didn't feel like a baby at all; in fact she felt more mature than before. The counselor was a good listener and didn't judge her or try to tell her what to do. She helped Hannah find her own answers in her own way.

for you to do

The situations below are all reasons why people have talked to counselors. Next to each, write the names of anyone you know who you think might have experienced this.

not liking oneself	
parents divorcing	
not getting along with family members	
grades dropping	
having angry outbursts	
feeling lonely	
feeling too shy	
feeling depressed	
abusing alcohol or drugs	
feeling afraid of the future	
feeling afraid to fly in an airplane	
wanting to stop smoking	
wanting to get along better with a friend	
feeling too stressed	
being unable to sleep	
eating too much or too little	
being physically or emotionally abused	
grief when a loved one dies	

Any of these situations can occur naturally in someone's life. Having these experiences does not make someone good or bad, smart or stupid, right or wrong. List any other reasons you can think of that someone might want to talk to a counselor.

_____

_____

_____

_____

...and more to do!

A counselor is a professional trained to help others. When someone goes to a counselor for help, it is a sign of wisdom, not weakness. Next to each occupation below, tell what might happen if people did not go to these professionals for help.

firefighter _____

medical doctor _____

teacher _____

athletic coach _____

police officer _____

physical therapist _____

college counselor _____

dentist _____

auto mechanic _____

computer technician _____

In your own words, explain what you think this statement means: Going to a counselor is a sign of wisdom, not weakness.

_____

_____

_____

_____

Why do you think Hannah could not get over her sadness by herself?

_____

_____

_____

What changed when she started talking to the counselor?

_____

_____

_____

Describe any situations you know of where someone's life is being negatively affected because they are not facing their problems.

_____

_____

_____

Describe any situations you know of where someone's life is being positively affected because they are facing their problems.

_____

_____

_____

How would you feel about talking to a counselor about your parents' divorce?

_____

_____

_____

31 group support

for you to know

Many teens find support by participating in a group designed to help them deal with divorce. The group usually has an adult leader and its student members all have parents in some stage of divorce. Sharing and listening in a support group can help you understand that you are not alone and can teach you new ways to cope with your experience.

Mrs. Carlson's divorce support group met every Wednesday afternoon in the guidance office. Between five and ten students showed up each week to share their experiences.

Mia's parents had been divorced for six months. Mia was having a hard time dealing with her mother, who was already engaged to another man.

Sam's parents were just starting divorce proceedings. They still lived together and argued a lot. They slammed doors when they were angry and sometimes left the house late at night. Their behavior scared both Sam and his younger sister.

Paula's parents' divorce would be final in two weeks. Her father had already moved out into a new apartment. She missed him very much and often felt sad.

Zach and Heather's parents had been divorced for a year. Zach lived with their father and Heather lived with their mother. Their parents often talked negatively about each other, blaming each other for the problems that were still going on despite their separation.

While each of the students' situations was a little different from the others, they all shared similar feelings of frustration, helplessness, sadness, and anger. Each week they shared their stories with each other, and with Mrs. Carlson's guidance, they helped each other learn ways to cope with their situations. The students in the group felt relieved that they had a place to share their stories with other kids who understood what they were going through. They found their parents' situations were easier to handle when they talked about them and had their feelings respected and validated.

for you to do

Pretend you are present at a meeting of Mrs. Carlson's support group. After each comment, tell how hearing it might make you feel and what you might say in response. It is important to know that you always have the option of just listening respectfully and not saying anything.

Mia: "I don't like the man my mother is dating. He tries to be nice to me but it hurts me to see her with him. I wish she would get back together with my father."

When I hear Mia say this, I might feel: _____

I might say: _____

Sam: "I hate it when my parents fight. Sometimes I'm afraid they might hurt each other."

When I hear Sam say this, I might feel: _____

I might say: _____

Paula: "I miss my dad so much. We used to spend so much time together, and now there are only weekends."

When I hear Paula say this, I might feel: _____

I might say: _____

Zach: "I hate it when my mom says bad things about my dad. It's like she wants me to agree with her that everything is his fault. I feel like I can't tell her that I love him, too."

When I hear Zach say this, I might feel: _____

I might say: _____

Heather: "I wish we all still lived together as one family instead of two."

When I hear Heather say this, I might feel: _____

I might say: _____

...and more to do!

Do you think you would feel comfortable being part of a support group for teens whose parents are divorcing? Explain your answer.

_____

_____

_____

_____

Tell what thoughts, feelings, or facts you might want to share with the group about your own situation.

_____

_____

_____

_____

Tell anything that you think you would not be comfortable sharing with a group.

_____

_____

_____

_____

What do you think group members might say in response to the information that you would share?

_____

_____

_____

_____

How would you want the group to respond to this information?

_____

_____

_____

_____

What do you think might be helpful to you about being part of a support group?

_____

_____

_____

_____

If you would like to try attending a support group meeting, ask a counselor, teacher, coach, parent, or other adult whom you trust to help you find a group that meets in your school or your town.

for you to know

An adult doesn't have to be a professional counselor to help support you through your parents' divorce. Any adult whom you know well enough and trust may be willing to listen to your thoughts and feelings, and may be able to offer suggestions to help you cope.

Chris talked about his home situation with his uncle, whom he had been close to since he was a little boy.

Ashley babysat for her neighbor down the block for three years. She felt comfortable with Mrs. Jens and sometimes talked to her about how she was feeling about her parents' divorce.

Adam would sometimes stay after football practice and talk to his coach about what was happening with his parents.

Sheena did volunteer work at the hospital, and the head nurse on her floor was kind and easy to talk to. She found herself sharing her difficult feelings about her parents' divorce with this woman.

Caroline had a good rapport with her English teacher this year. Ms. Stephanos told Caroline that she could stay after school to talk whenever she needed to.

for you to do

After each of the words below, write the name of someone you know who plays this role in your life.

Friendly neighbor _____

Aunt _____

Grandmother _____

Coach _____

Classroom teacher _____

Other helpful teacher _____

Uncle _____

Scout leader _____

Employer _____

Grandfather _____

Family friend _____

Spiritual leader _____

Put at star next to any of these people whom you might feel comfortable asking for support.

Add the names of any other adults you might feel comfortable asking for support.

_____

_____

_____

...and more to do!

Write the names of three adults you have identified who might support you.

After each name, fill in the details about your relationship with this person.

Name

_____

How we met

_____

How long I have known them

_____

How often I see them

_____

What I like about them

_____

Why I feel comfortable with them

_____

Why I trust them

_____

Why they would support me

_____

Their phone number

_____

Their e-mail address

_____

activity 32 ✶ getting help from adults you trust

Name

How we met

How long I have known them

How often I see them

What I like about them

Why I feel comfortable with them

Why I trust them

Why they would support me

Their phone number

Their e-mail address

Name

_____

How we met

_____

How long I have known them

_____

How often I see them

_____

What I like about them

_____

Why I feel comfortable with them

_____

Why I trust them

_____

Why they would support me

_____

Their phone number

_____

Their e-mail address

_____

If you are feeling the need for support right now, choose one of these people and plan a time when you will contact them. Write your plan here.

_____

_____

_____

_____

Describe what it will feel like for you to contact this person.

_____

_____

_____

_____

Explain how you think they will respond to your request for support.

_____

_____

_____

_____

you to know

divorce, one parent is so angry or hurt that
their teen to turn away from the other parent
to them. No matter what happens between
ve the right to love both of them and to remain

Kurt didn't know what to do. When he was with his mom, she told him lots of negative stories about his dad—things that his dad had done over the years that she didn't like. She always ended up asking Kurt, "You can see what a jerk your father is, can't you?" Kurt didn't know what to say. He loved his father, even if his dad had made some mistakes and behaved poorly sometimes.

When Kurt was with his father, his dad continually complained about Kurt's mother. He called her names and told Kurt she was nutty. He said he didn't know how Kurt could stand living with her. He'd ask, "You can see why I had to get away from her, can't you?" Again, Kurt didn't know what to say. He knew his mom could be difficult to get along with at times, but he loved her very much. He didn't want to take sides with his dad against her.

Kurt hated the position his parents put him in. He knew neither of them was perfect, but they were his parents and he loved them both. If he agreed with one about how bad the other was, he felt terribly guilty. If he didn't agree, he felt guilty as well. He didn't know how to please them both without hurting one or the other. He was beginning to feel stressed whenever he was with either of them because he knew the conversation that was coming.

One day Kurt's grandfather was visiting. He was present when Kurt's mom asked Kurt to agree that his father was a loser. His grandfather told Kurt's mother that he was upset by this conversation. She became angry and walked out of the room. When that happened, Kurt's grandfather told him that he never had to take sides against his father, or his mother either for that matter. Kurt told him what was happening with both of his parents, and how uncomfortable it made him feel. His grandfather said he'd talk to his mother about it again, and in the meantime, Kurt must learn to say to his parents: "Please don't ask me to take sides. You are both my parents and I have the right to love you both."

r you to do

s' names on the shirts of the teen and parents in
nversation balloon, write something negative that
he other. Then, in your conversation balloons,
ask me to take sides. You are both my parents and I
)r, write words of your own choice that convey the

...and more to do!

Describe what it feels like when one parent tries to get you to take sides against the other.

_____

_____

_____

_____

Describe any attempts you have already made to get your parents to stop doing this.

_____

_____

_____

_____

Tell what it feels like to look at the pictures of yourself asking for your parents to respect your right to love them both.

_____

_____

_____

_____

Tell what you think would happen if you actually spoke these words to your mother.

_____

_____

_____

_____

_____

Tell what you think would happen if you actually spoke these words to your father.

_____

_____

_____

_____

_____

If you feel concerned about stating your rights to either of your parents, you might try two things to make it easier:

1. Rehearse what you will say beforehand, either by yourself or with someone else.

2. Ask another adult whom you trust to be present when you talk to your parents.

3. Talk to your parents in a counselor's office with a counselor present to help your family members communicate clearly and peacefully.

34 your right to remain separate from parental problems

for you to know

If your parents have problems in their relationship, these problems are their responsibility—not yours. Sometimes parents try to draw teens into the middle of their relationship or their problems. You have the right to remain separate from your parents' problems.

Michelle felt like she was living in a war zone. She thought the fighting would stop once her parents got divorced, but it had just changed its pattern. She no longer had to listen to them argue at home, but now she felt like she was a pawn in their battle plan. Often when her mother was angry at her father, she wouldn't let Michelle visit him. When her dad was angry with her mom, he would say things like: "Tell your mother she'd better come up with that money she owes me, or she'll be sorry." Sometimes Michelle would try to work things out between her parents; she would tell them nice things about each other or try to give them suggestions on how to work out their problems. None of this helped, and it only made Michelle feel frustrated and drained. When she was put in the middle of her parents' conflict, she felt used and hurt.

One Friday afternoon, Michelle got a stomachache during her last class. It was so bad that the teacher excused her to go to the nurse's office. The nurse pushed gently in a few places around Michelle's stomach. She said she didn't feel anything unusual, and asked Michelle if she'd eaten anything different or if there was anything bothering her. Michelle told her she was worried about going to her dad's for the weekend, and she explained to the nurse about feeling caught in the middle of her parents' conflict. The nurse said that sometimes worry and tension can cause stomachaches. She told Michelle that she had the right to stay separate from her parents' problems and they needed to understand this.

The nurse set up a meeting with Michelle and her parents for the next week. She explained to them that putting Michelle in the middle of their conflict was not fair to her and was becoming harmful to her health. Their problems were their responsibility, and they needed to work them out by themselves. Michelle's parents listened to the nurse and apologized to Michelle. They hadn't realized how they were using her to send negative messages to each other. They agreed to work on changing this and to meet with the nurse again in a month to see if things had improved.

Michelle's parents had a hard time changing their ways, but they kept trying and eventually things got better. When they went back to their old habits, Michelle would point to her stomach to remind them of their promise.

for you to do

Write your name in the center column and one parent's name in each column on the sides. On the lines underneath each parent's name, write the "weapons"—the words or behaviors—that parent uses to put you in the middle of the relationship. On the lines underneath your name, describe how you feel when they do this.

_____   _____   _____

_____   _____   _____

_____   _____   _____

_____   _____   _____

_____   _____   _____

_____   _____   _____

_____   _____   _____

In the conversation balloon, write words you could use to tell your parents what they are doing to you and to ask them to stop.

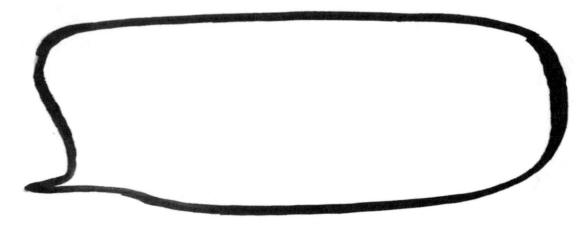

...and more to do!

Why do you think Michelle was getting stomachaches?

_____

_____

_____

_____

Describe how being in the middle of your parents' conflict affects you emotionally.

_____

_____

_____

_____

Describe how being in the middle of your parents' conflict affects you physically.

_____

_____

_____

_____

Rewrite the following statement in your own handwriting: *"I have the right to stay separate from my parents' conflicts and problems."*

_____

_____

Describe how it would feel for you to tell your parents to stop putting you in the middle of their problems.

_____

_____

_____

_____

_____

Make a plan to tell your parents how you feel. If you think it might be hard to bring this up, show them this exercise to help explain what you are feeling and thinking. If it is still too difficult, talk to a counselor or other adult about helping you.

your right to remain a teen

for you to know

When parents divorce and then live without an adult partner, they may begin to treat their teen as another adult rather than their child. This puts teens in an inappropriate position. You have the right to remain in a child's role in your relationship with your parents.

When Matt's parents divorced and his father moved out, Matt's mother told him, "Well, honey, you're the man of the house now." Matt wasn't sure what that meant at first, but soon he found out. Matt's mother began relying on him to help discipline his younger siblings. Matt was not comfortable with this responsibility. He was only a few years older than his brother and felt uneasy being put into a father role. His mother also started borrowing money from Matt occasionally. Matt would have to dig into the money he'd saved from his summer job. His mom told him she'd pay him back, but she never did. This made Matt feel angry and betrayed.

When Kera's parents got divorced, Kera's father moved out of the state. Kera visited him during school vacations, and she was usually there for a week or more. Kera's dad started talking to her differently. He shared a lot of information about his business problems, and also about problems in his relationship with his new girlfriend. One night he took Kera out to a bar after work with his coworkers. He didn't allow her to drink alcohol, but he included her in the adult conversations. Kera did not feel good in these situations. She was uncomfortable and nervous. She didn't want to have this grown-up relationship with her father; she wanted him to act like a father again.

Both Matt's mother and Kera's father put their teens into positions that were not appropriate. While teens can help by babysitting or doing chores around the house, it is not their job to take on parental duties. While parents can share some information about their personal lives with their teens, it is not appropriate to treat their teens as peers. Teens are more grown-up than grade-school children, but it is not their job to replace one parent in the other parent's life.

for you to do

Parents don't always realize that their actions are hurting their teens, so they need to be made aware of what going on. One way of doing this is for teens to explain how they feel.

Fill in the blanks in these statements explaining what Matt and Kera might say to their parents to make them understand.

Mom, when you _____

_____, I feel

_____

_____

_____

Dad, when you _____

_____, I feel

_____

_____

_____

...and more to do!

Describe any situations where your mom or dad inappropriately put you in the role of an adult.

_____

_____

_____

_____

Explain how this made you feel and why.

_____

_____

_____

_____

Fill in the blanks below to create statements that could help your parents understand how you feel.

Mom, when you _____

_____, I feel

_____

Dad, when you _____

_____, I feel

_____

Mom, when you _____

_____, I feel

_____

Dad, when you _____

_____, I feel

_____

What do you think it would be like to say this to your parents?

_____

_____

_____

_____

How do you think they might respond?

_____

_____

_____

_____

If you don't think you could tell your parents how you feel, tell a counselor or other adult. Talk about whether that adult could help you tell your parents.

for you to know

Sometimes when parents get divorced, they become very wrapped up in their own situations and begin to neglect some of their parenting duties. No matter what is happening in your parents' lives, it is your right to be provided with adequate parental care.

Jose was pretty self-sufficient. He could come home to an empty house, get his homework done, and make some dinner for himself and his younger sister without any problem. But since his parents got divorced, he was beginning to feel neglected. Sometimes when he wanted to make dinner there wasn't any food in the refrigerator. His mother would pick up something from a restaurant on her way home from work, but often that wasn't until eight o'clock at night.

Jose also missed getting help with his science homework from his dad on weeknights. He would see his dad on Saturdays, but frequently that was too late. He had tried calling his dad on the phone, but he and his new wife had just had twin babies, and his dad just didn't seem to have much time to help Jose.

When Jose's little sister had her first dance recital, neither of their parents had time to go see her perform. Jose knew his sister was very hurt, but he didn't know what to do. Finally he talked to his counselor at school. The counselor told Jose that his parents needed to find time to take better care of Jose and his sister. He set up a meeting with the family, and they all discussed the situation. The counselor told Jose's parents that no matter how busy they were, they needed to care for all of their children adequately. He helped them think of ways that they could be more responsible with this, and after a while things improved. Jose was glad he had asked for help.

activity 36 ✳ your right to be parented

for you to do

The checklist below shows responsibilities that parents have in caring for their children. Add any other responsibilities that you think are important that are not listed. (It is important to differentiate between life necessities and luxuries. Personal phones, cars, and televisions are examples of luxuries; they are not necessary items for parents to provide.) Then check the appropriate boxes and explain your choice under "Comments" to show what is happening in your family.

My Household

Parents' Responsibility	Provided/Not Provided		Comments
food			
clothing			
shelter			
education			
health care			
clean home			
discipline			
emotional support			
adult supervision			
homework help			
transportation			
encouragement			
advice			
love			
other:			
other:			

...and more to do!

List each item that you have checked as "not provided" and then tell how not having this affects you.

_____

_____

_____

_____

_____

Explain why you think your mother or father might not be providing everything you need at this time.

_____

_____

_____

_____

Do you think your parents are aware of the responsibilities they are neglecting? Explain your answer.

_____

_____

_____

_____

Check which of the actions below you might take to let your parents know how you feel and what you need:

☐ Talk to them by yourself.

☐ Show them this exercise.

☐ Write them a letter.

☐ Ask a family member to talk to them with you.

☐ Ask a family friend to talk to them with you.

☐ Ask a counselor or teacher to talk to them with you.

☐ Ask a spiritual leader to talk to them with you.

☐ Ask another adult whom you trust to talk to them with you.

☐ Other: _____

It is important that your parents know which of your needs are not being met. If they don't know, they can't help you. Describe when and where you can let your parents know how you feel and what you need, and which of the above actions you will take.

_____

_____

_____

_____

Make sure to follow through with your plan.

your right to stay in contact 37
with extended family

for you to know

Sometimes when parents divorce, a teen's contact with their extended family members gets cut off. Parents' problems shouldn't interfere with a teen's relationships. You have the right to continue appropriate relationships with any members of your extended family that you choose.

A nuclear family consists of parents and children. An extended family encompasses additional family members, such as grandparents, aunts, uncles, and cousins. Some extended families also include people who are not actually related by blood, but are so close emotionally that they feel like part of the family.

Both nuclear family members and extended family members are important parts of a teen's life. You can receive nurturing, guidance, support, friendship, and fun from relationships with all of your family members.

When parents divorce, sometimes relationships with extended family members either become more limited or are cut off altogether. One parent may not want their teen to continue seeing the other parent's relatives, or one parent's family may be angry at the other parent due to circumstances of the divorce. No matter what happens between the divorcing parents, teens should always be allowed to continue contact with their extended family, as long as it is safe and appropriate.

for you to do

In the box below, draw a tree with extending branches. Write your name, draw your face, or paste a picture of yourself on its trunk. On the branches, do the same with the members of your nuclear family and extended family in the appropriate places. On the lines below, write the names of those who are not blood relatives, but whom you consider to be part of your extended family because you are so close to them. When you are done, put a star next to the members of your extended family with whom you would like to maintain a relationship.

_____   _____   _____

_____   _____   _____

_____   _____   _____

...and more to do!

List the names of any starred family members with whom you have had little or no contact because of your parents' divorce. Next to each name, tell what you like or miss most about that person.

_____

_____

_____

Do you think your parents are aware of your desire to have more contact with these people? Explain why.

_____

_____

_____

Write the words you could use to tell your parents how you feel and what you would like to be different.

_____

_____

_____

Tell how you think your parents might respond to your words. Explain what you think they might say and what actions you think they might take in response.

_____

_____

_____

Plan a time to talk to your parents about this. If you are not comfortable talking to them by yourself, ask a counselor or other adult whom you trust to talk to them with you.

38 your right to separate from your family

Kirsten felt that she was backsliding in her life. When her parents got divorced, it seemed that something changed inside her. Sometimes she felt that she shouldn't go out with her friends because her mom would be left at home alone. Sometimes she wanted to go to the lake with her boyfriend and his family instead of seeing her dad on the weekend, but she knew her dad would be alone and didn't want to disappoint him. Sometimes when she thought about going away to college, she wondered if it would be too hard on her mom to be so far away from her.

Kirsten felt a desire to spend more time with her friends, to get a job, and to make more decisions on her own. But with her parents split up, she also felt like they needed her more. Even her younger sister seemed to want to spend more time with Kirsten and had become more emotionally attached to her. Kirsten didn't know how she was supposed to live her own life and take care of her family's needs at the same time.

Kirsten brought up this subject in her health class when they were talking about stages of human development. Kirsten said she thought she had been developing normally until her parents got divorced, but now she felt like her family was keeping her from becoming more independent. The health teacher said it made sense that Kirsten felt that way considering what was happening. He also said it was important that Kirsten realize it was her right to go on with her life despite her parents' divorce. She could continue to be loving and caring to her family, but she could not fill all their emotional needs for them.

for you to do

In the column on the left, write words or phrases that describe what you are doing or would like to do to become more independent. In the column on the right, write what your family might be doing that you feel prevents you from becoming independent; then circle the phrases in this column that you think are a result of your parents' divorce.

Becoming More Independent

_____

_____

_____

_____

_____

_____

_____

_____

_____

_____

Preventing My Independence

_____

_____

_____

_____

_____

_____

_____

_____

_____

_____

...and more to do!

Explain the phrases that you circled in more detail.

_____

_____

_____

_____

_____

_____

Explain how each of these situations might be different if your parents hadn't gotten divorced.

_____

_____

_____

_____

_____

Talk with a counselor or another adult about each of the ways you would like to be more independent. Discuss whether your ideas are appropriate and safe for your age and maturity level. Put a check mark next to those ideas that are appropriate and an X next to those that are not appropriate.

Tell how you think your parents would respond if you talked to them about the appropriate ways in which you would like to be more independent.

_____

_____

_____

_____

_____

_____

Describe ways that you can still be loving and caring to your family without letting them keep you from becoming independent.

_____

_____

_____

_____

_____

_____

Plan a time that you can talk to your parents about what you have written in this exercise. If you are not comfortable talking to them alone, ask a counselor or other adult whom you trust to be with you.

39 if one parent is far away

for you to know

Sometimes when parents divorce, one parent moves a great distance away, making it more difficult to see that parent often. However, this does not have to hinder the relationship. There are many ways for a parent and teen to maintain a close relationship despite the amount of physical distance between them.

When Allie's parents got divorced, her mother told her she was moving out of town. She had gotten an important job that would allow her to pay Allie's dad to care for Allie and also pay for Allie's college education. But the job was far away and took up a lot of time. Allie was upset. She was afraid she would either never see her mom again, or that her mom might forget about her altogether. Allie told her mom about these fears, and her mother told her that she would not allow this to happen.

To help reassure Allie, her mom got out a calendar and a map, and the two of them spent one afternoon planning how they could stay close despite the physical distance. They figured out how long it would take to either drive or fly to where Allie's mom was moving, as well as the bus and train routes between both homes. When Allie realized she could be at her mom's house in less than an hour by plane, she felt a little better. They also determined the halfway point between them and learned that it was a nice town with some good hotels, a shopping mall, and a water park. Her dad agreed to drive Allie there if she and her mom wanted to meet for a weekend.

Allie and her mom also talked about how they would keep in touch on a daily and weekly basis. They both had cell phones and e-mail, so they agreed to start off by e-mailing each morning and calling each night after dinner. On the nights Allie had drama club, she would call her mom a little later. Allie's mom made sure their phone package was set up so they each had free minutes when they called each other.

Allie's mom also called Allie's school and let them know that she wanted to be on the contact list about Allie's grades, behaviors, and school activities. She wrote in all the dates of Allie's drama performances so she could get off work ahead of time and come to see them. They planned their first weekend together for two weeks from the time that Allie's mom moved. They also marked the dates on the calendar that Allie's mom would be in town on business, so they could spend time together. They even talked about the next school break and the following summer when Allie would come and stay with her mom for long periods of time.

By the end of the afternoon Allie felt much better. She was glad she had told her mom about her fears, and she felt very confident that she and her mom could keep up a close relationship even over a long distance. Allie knew she would miss seeing her mom every day, but she also knew that the separation wasn't as bad as she had first thought it would be.

for you to do

The list below includes several means of keeping in touch with someone. Describe how you would ideally like to use each one to stay in touch with your distant parent. Include how often you would like to use each. Then transfer your answers to the blank calendar to show a typical two-month period.

E-mail _____

Telephone _____

Fax _____

Pager _____

Postal service _____

Car _____

Taxicab _____

Bus _____

Train _____

Airline _____

Put a plus sign by the parts of this plan you think are actually possible, and a minus sign by those that are not. Explain your choices here.

_____

_____

_____

...and more to do!

Think back to the time when you first learned that your parent was moving away. Describe where you were and tell what was said. Explain how you felt when you heard this news.

_____

_____

_____

_____

Explain what is the hardest part of having your parent far away.

_____

_____

_____

Tell why you think your parent made the decision to move away.

_____

_____

_____

Do you think your parent made a wise decision in moving away? Explain your answer.

_____

_____

_____

_____

Tell whether you think you have enough contact with your distant parent. What, if anything, would you like to change about your arrangement?

_____

_____

_____

_____

If you do not feel you have enough contact with your distant parent, make a plan to talk to them about this. Think about where, when, and how you will do this. Describe your plan here.

_____

_____

_____

_____

If you are uncomfortable talking to your parent about your feelings, show them this exercise or ask a counselor or other adult to help you.

40 if one parent leaves you

for you to know

Sometimes one parent feels so extremely hurt or emotionally damaged by a divorce, they believe that the only way for them to recover is to escape from their current life. Parents who have few or no healthy coping skills may leave their job, their home, and even their children to try to help themselves feel better. If a parent leaves a teen's life, it is never the teen's fault.

When Ebony's parents divorced, her father told her he would call her a lot to keep in touch and she could visit him every weekend. The first two weekends, Ebony stayed with her dad at his brother Bob's house. The next weekend, her dad called to say he was looking for an apartment and couldn't pick her up. The weekend after that, he called to say he had gone on a trip and would call her when he got back. Ebony didn't hear from her father again for over a year. She felt hurt and betrayed. She wondered what she had done wrong to make him stop loving her or not want to be with her.

Uncle Bob tried to explain to Ebony that her dad's absence had nothing to do with her. He said that her dad was very unhappy with his life and kept trying to get away from his unhappiness by going to new places. He also said that her dad had to learn how to deal with his sadness instead of trying to run away from it. Unfortunately, even though it had nothing to do with her, her dad's problem hurt Ebony very much.

Ebony found that talking to Uncle Bob about her dad helped her feel a little better. Both of them loved her dad and hoped that he would come home soon. Uncle Bob helped Ebony to understand her dad better. It also felt nice to share happy memories about her dad with someone else who loved him. Eventually Ebony was able to see that her dad's leaving didn't have anything to do with her relationship with him; it had to do with his relationship with himself.

for you to do

On the notebook page below, write a letter to the parent who has left you, telling them how you feel about them being gone. (Use more paper if you need to.) You can choose whether to actually send this letter or not.

	Dear
◯	
◯	
◯	

...and more to do!

Describe what you miss most about your absent parent.

_____

_____

_____

_____

_____

Tell what the hardest part is about having this parent absent from your life.

_____

_____

_____

Explain why you would or would not send the letter that you wrote.

_____

_____

_____

Just as with Ebony's father, when any parent leaves, it is because they are having trouble with their relationship with themselves. Tell what you think might have been troubling your own parent to make them leave.

_____

_____

_____

It can be hard to think of a parent as a person with problems that they can't solve.
Explain why you think this is so hard.

_____

_____

_____

_____

_____

_____

Do you think it might help you to talk to someone else about your absent parent the
way Ebony talked to her uncle Bob? Explain your answer.

_____

_____

_____

_____

_____

Share your letter, or your thoughts and feelings, with a counselor, or someone else
whom you trust.

41 when a parent needs help

for you to know

Divorce is rarely easy, but sometimes it can wound a parent so deeply that they have trouble continuing to function in healthy ways. Parents who cannot maintain their responsibilities to their jobs or families or whose behavior may hurt themselves or others can get help from professional counselors and doctors.

Since his parents got divorced, Jared's mom was sleeping more and more. Sometimes she didn't go to work, and Jared would find her sleeping on the couch when he got home from school. Sometimes there were empty vodka bottles next to her or in the sink. One day Jared came home and there was no electricity in his house—his mom hadn't paid the bill.

Since her parents got divorced, Beth's father seemed very angry. She rarely saw him smile, and sometimes he yelled at her so loudly that she felt afraid. Once when he was mad she saw him kick a large garbage can across the driveway, and garbage flew everywhere. Then he got into his car and pulled out of the driveway, driving very fast. Beth's mother saw what happened and said the court wouldn't let Beth visit her dad if he couldn't control his temper.

Both Jared and Beth went to divorce support group meetings at the community counseling center. One day Jared told the group about his mom's behavior and said that he was afraid she would lose her job. Caroline, the group leader, asked if any other teens had parents whose behaviors were extreme or frightening. Beth raised her hand and told about how intense her father's temper had gotten.

Caroline explained to the group that sometimes parents feel so bad that they cannot handle their deep feelings in healthy ways. When their behavior becomes dangerous to themselves or others, they need to get help. It is important that teens who see these behaviors tell someone who can get help for their parents. Caroline helped Jared's mom get an evaluation for substance abuse treatment. She helped Beth's dad sign up for a class in anger management.

for you to do

The following chart lists unhealthy ways to cope with pain. Check which behaviors can be dangerous to oneself, which can be dangerous to others, which could prevent someone from doing their job, and which could prevent someone from caring for their family. Add any more behaviors you know of that are not on this list.

	dangerous to oneself	dangerous to others	prevent someone from doing their job	prevent someone from caring for their family
Expressing anger violently	☐	☐	☐	☐
Using street drugs	☐	☐	☐	☐
Using alcohol	☐	☐	☐	☐
Being severely depressed	☐	☐	☐	☐
Not eating enough	☐	☐	☐	☐
Abusing prescription drugs	☐	☐	☐	☐
Being sexually promiscuous	☐	☐	☐	☐
Being severely anxious	☐	☐	☐	☐
Doing physically reckless activities	☐	☐	☐	☐
Other _____	☐	☐	☐	☐
Other _____	☐	☐	☐	☐
Other _____	☐	☐	☐	☐

Explain when and where you have seen any of these behaviors in either of your parents.

_____

_____

_____

_____

Tell how your parent's behavior has affected you.

_____

_____

_____

_____

_____

_____

_____

...and more to do!

If you have witnessed dangerous behaviors in either of your parents, it is important that they get help. Circle any of the following people who might assist your parent in getting the help they need.

physician	counselor	grandparent	teacher
spiritual leader	aunt or uncle	friend	neighbor

Who else could help your parent?

_____

It can be very difficult having a parent who needs help. If your parent needs help, you may need support as well. Tell who you could ask for help for yourself

_____

Make a plan to ask for help for both your parent and yourself. Explain who you will ask, where, and when you will ask them. Then be sure to follow through.

	Help for my parent	Help for myself
Who		
Where		
When		

42 possible positives

for you to know

Many teenagers who have lived through their parents' divorce can identify positive ways that the experience affected their lives. This might be hard to believe at first, but as with any life challenge, if you view it from the right angle you can eventually identify something positive that you gained from the experience.

Sarah was fourteen when her parents got divorced. She felt it was the worst thing that could ever happen. She hated having to miss social activities when she visited her father on the weekends, and she hated having to babysit for her younger brother after school when her mother started working. She hated how sad she felt all the time, and she was angry at her parents for ruining her life.

It took Sarah a long time to get past her feelings of sadness and resentment. Talking to a counselor helped, and so did keeping a journal where she wrote out her feelings of anger and loss. During Sarah's senior year in high school, she was asked to show a new student around the school. The new girl, Emily, had to move to a smaller house in a different school district because her parents had gotten divorced. Emily confided to Sarah how upsetting the divorce was to her.

As Sarah listened, she realized she could empathize with Emily's feelings. Sarah also realized something else. She found herself telling Emily some positive things that had come from her parents' divorce—like how nice it was to not have to listen to her parents' loud arguments all the time; how she had gotten to know her father better when they spent time together on the weekends; how she and her brother had gotten closer by sharing their sadness about the divorce; and how much stronger she had grown emotionally by having to go through the experience. Now when she had disappointments in her life, she knew that she could get through them because she had survived one of the hardest ones of all—her parents splitting up.

for you to do

Circle any of the phrases below that describe something you have experienced in your life that might have appeared difficult at first.

learning to walk	starting kindergarten	learning to swim
learning to skate	learning to tie your shoes	learning to drive
learning to ride a bike	having a pet die	losing a friend
moving to a new house	starting a new school	playing a sport
passing a hard class	passing a hard test	apologizing
trying out for a play	giving an oral report	asking for a date
a loved one's death	breaking up a romance	a loved one's illness

Choose one or more of the items you circled and write about how this experience, while difficult at first, ended up bringing something positive to your life.

_____

_____

_____

_____

_____

...and more to do!

Read the story about Sarah and Emily one more time. Do you think it is realistic that Sarah eventually found something positive in her parents' divorce? Explain your answer.

_____

_____

_____

_____

Describe some of the challenges Emily will face as her parents divorce and she moves and has to start a new school.

_____

_____

_____

Make a guess as to what positives might come from Emily's experience.

_____

_____

_____

_____

Tell how your own situation is similar to or different from Sarah's and Emily's.

_____

_____

_____

_____

_____

_____

Pretend it is five years into the future. Write the number of the year and how old you will be, and tell what positives you might see as you look back on your experience with your parents' divorce.

_____

_____

_____

_____

_____

_____

_____

_____

Lisa M. Schab, LCSW, is a licensed clinical social worker with a private counseling practice in the Chicago suburbs. She writes a monthly parenting column for *Chicago Parent* magazine and is the author of eight self-help books and workbooks for children and adults. Schab teaches self-help and relaxation therapy workshops for the general public and professional training courses for therapists. She received her bachelor's degree from Northwestern University and her master's degree in clinical social work from Loyola University.